DRUGS the facts about
DRUGS AND SOCIETY

DRUGS the facts about

DRUGS AND SOCIETY

JOAN AXELROD-CONTRADA

Marshall Cavendish
Benchmark

New York

For my parents, who encouraged my interest in current events

Acknowledgment
Thanks to John Roll, PhD, Director, Washington Institute for Mental Illness Research and
Training, Washington State University, for his expert review of this manuscript.

Marshall Cavendish Benchmark
99 White Plains Road
Tarrytown, NY 10591
www.marshallcavendish.us

Library of Congress Cataloging-in-Publication Data

Axelrod-Contrada, Joan.
Drug abuse and society / by Joan Axelrod-Contrada.
p. cm. — (Drugs)
Includes bibliographical references and index.
ISBN 978-0-7614-2674-5
1. Drug abuse—Juvenile literature. 2. Drug abuse—
Social aspects—Juvenile literature. 3. Drugs and popular music—
Juvenile literature. I. Title. II. Series.

HV5801.A94 2007
362.29—dc22

2007002261

Medical Illustration on p. 65: Ian Worpole

Photo Research by Joan Meisel

Cover photo: Colin Anderson

The photographs in this book are used by the courtesy of:
Cover photo: Brand X Pictures/Alamy
AP Images: 30, 37, 77, 100; Alamy: 1, 2-3, Brand X Pictures; 6, Mark
Hamilton; 14, The Print Collector; 20, Classic Image; 56, 80, Jeff
Greenberg; 62, Scott Camazine; 72, Robert Harding Picture Library
Ltd; 86, Comstock Images; Corbis: 42, Ole Graf; Everett Collection:
39, WB/Courtesy: Everett Collection; Photo Researchers, Inc.: 54,
Cordelia Molloy

Publisher: Michelle Bisson
Art Director: Anahid Hamparian
Series Designer: Sonia Chaghatzbanian

Printed in Malaysia

1 3 5 6 4 2

CONTENTS

LEGAL AND ILLEGAL DRUGS ARE PART OF EVERYDAY LIFE WHEREVER PEOPLE LOOK.

INTRODUCTION

Just Say Know

Increasingly, this phrase is taking the place of the old antidrug slogan "Just Say No." The new thinking recognizes the complexity of drug abuse. To "just say know" means to understand how legal and illegal drugs affect not only the human body, but also society at large. Every day, families are torn apart, employers lose valuable workers, crime devastates communities, and people die—all as a result of drug abuse.

The term "drug abuse" has two meanings—one legal, the other psychiatric. While legally the use of any illegal substance is "abuse," psychiatrists define abuse as occurring when users put themselves or others at risk. Most people who use drugs, such as alcohol and marijuana, do not cross the line into abuse. However, those who do cost society billions of dollars in crime, lost productivity, and health care costs.

Even the so-called "legal drugs" (at least for adults) cause problems, too. A drug is any substance that, in small amounts, changes the way the body or mind works. Nicotine, for example, is a legal substance for those over the age of eighteen. Yet this stimulant is highly addictive and may lead to serious health problems. About one in three smokers dies of the long-term effects of tobacco.

Alcohol is a complex legal drug for those over twenty-one. Although a depressant, it can also fuel aggression. As the oldest and most widely used drug in the world, it exacts more of a toll on society than that of all illegal drugs combined. Excessive drinking can lead to car crashes, failed relationships, and lost jobs.

Some young people use easily available household products, such as glue and air freshener, to get high. When used as inhalants, these products can also be considered drugs, because they change the ways the body and the mind work. Inhalants can trigger Sudden Sniffing Death Syndrome, a failure of the heart or lungs. Inhalants are particularly popular with some risk-taking young teenagers because of their low cost and easy availability.

Researchers also have noticed an increase in the number of young people abusing prescription drugs, such as OxyContin and Ritalin. OxyContin, which is sometimes called "hillbilly heroin," causes a state of drowsy euphoria much like heroin. Ritalin, in turn, has the paradoxical effect of calming patients with Attention Deficit Hyperactivity Disorder (ADHD) while stimulating those who do not have ADHD. Prescription drugs taken without a doctor's orders can cause the same damage as street drugs, although many people falsely believe they are safe.

Illegal drugs, such as marijuana and methamphetamine, cause their own sets of problems. First, because such drugs are unregulated, buyers rarely know exactly what they're getting. Second, people who use illegal drugs run the risk of being arrested or engaging in risky behavior. Marijuana is, by far, the most commonly used illegal drug. The relatively new stimulant methamphetamine has swept across America, attracting users from across the socioeconomic spectrum. Young people in both rural and suburban communities have been particularly vulnerable to its lure.

Researchers point to a complex array of individual, social, and biological factors that put some people more at risk than others of developing a problem with substances. A family background of substance abuse, for instance, makes someone more likely to develop a problem. Parents who are too strict or too lax may also contribute to drug abuse. Poor academic performance and poverty also influence drug use.

Peer preference, and not necessarily peer pressure, strongly influences whether someone will use drugs. Many young people freely choose to be part of a "partying" crowd where drug use is commonplace. Choosing hard-partying friends who socialize in settings where drug use is going on increases the chances that an individual will also begin using drugs.

Over the years, drugs have become stronger in response to new technologies and scientific discoveries. Chapter 1 (Drugs and History) details how cultural traditions that once controlled the use of substances have faded, leaving societies more open to the problems of drug abuse.

Some people blame pop culture for glamorizing drug use, but as indicated in Chapter 2 (Drugs and Pop Culture), the truth is more complex. Research shows that depictions in music, movies, and television vary by the substance. Even though "sex, drugs, and rock 'n' roll" often go together, rock songs do not always portray illegal drugs in a positive light. Many songs depict hard drugs such as heroin negatively. Numerous rock stars, including Anthony Kiedis of the Red Hot Chili Peppers and Steven Tyler of Aerosmith, have told their own cautionary tales of addiction.

Meanwhile, beer commercials on prime-time television equate drinking with popularity and fun. Cigarette companies promote their products at youth-oriented sporting events. The tobacco and alcohol industries also have come under fire for marketing candy-flavored cigarettes and sweet alcoholic drinks, products that appeal to underaged consumers. One study found that eight-to-twelve year olds could name more brands of beer than United States' presidents.

Most drug use, legal and illegal, takes place between the ages of fifteen and eighteen, as Chapter 3 (Drugs and Risk Factors) notes.

In general, males use more drugs than females; but as discussed in Chapter 4 (Drugs and Gender), teenage girls appear to be catching up to their brothers and male friends.

Gateway Drugs

A "gateway" drug is easier to define than to explain. By definition, it is any drug that appears to lead to the use of other drugs. To explain why some people move from one drug to a seemingly more potent one, some experts point to changes in brain chemistry that affect the way people respond to stress. Other experts believe that social and psychological factors are key. Even though most users of cigarettes, alcohol, and marijuana do not progress to more powerful mind-altering substances such as cocaine and heroin, those who do often began using addictive substances at an early age. A new theory points to cigarettes and beer as the true gateway drugs, since young people generally drink and smoke cigarettes before they try marijuana. While most young people who try marijuana never move on to other drugs, those who smoke pot before the age of fourteen have a greater chance of using other drugs than those who don't. Factors such as thrill-seeking behavior, trauma, and poverty make some people more vulnerable than others to the gateway effect.

In 2004, teenage girls started to outnumber teenage boys in their misuse of prescription drugs. The use of steroids, meanwhile, has spread from professional athletes to teenage boys who want to look like the action character G. I. Joe in much the same way that their sisters emulate the Barbie doll figure. Some observers link adolescent drug abuse to the culture's emphasis on sex and appearances to the detriment of self-esteem and self-confidence.

Biological factors, too, help explain why substance use sometimes escalates into abuse. Chapter 5 (Drugs and the Brain) describes how all addictive drugs, including alcohol and tobacco, hijack a part of the brain known as the "reward" or "pleasure" center.

Because of the dangers of drug abuse, governments pass laws to protect citizens. But are these laws prohibiting substances fair? Some people say yes, advocating a tough stance on illegal drugs. Others, who answer no, believe that certain drugs should be legalized. Chapter 6 (Drugs and the Law) explores the debate on drugs and the law. A growing number of people advocate a middle ground that favors treatment over punishment.

Drug courts that emphasize treatment over imprisonment have become a popular new option. However, they are not foolproof. Chapter 7 (Drugs and Treatment) describes the complexity of the recovery process. Among the most controversial forms of treatment: wilderness programs and "boot camps" for teenagers. Another concern is the question of whether teenagers without serious drug problems are taking treatment spots away from drug users who most need help.

Since drug abuse is such a costly problem, many people believe more efforts should be directed toward prevention. Chapter 8 (Drugs and Prevention) describes how school-based drug prevention programs are moving away from the fear-based messages and scare tactics of the past to messages that help teenagers meet the challenges of the present. How the "war on drugs" will be fought in the future remains to be seen. Teenagers who "just say know" undoubtedly will be part of the solution.

ANCIENT EGYPTIAN TOMB WALLS SHOW EVIDENCE OF GRAPE CULTIVATION AND
WINEMAKING, WHICH PROBABLY BEGAN AROUND 3000 BCE IN EGYPT.
ARCHAEOLOGISTS EXPLORING ROYAL TOMBS HAVE FOUND CONTAINERS THAT
ONCE HELD FOOD AND WINE FOR THE DECEASED TO CONSUME IN THE AFTERLIFE.

1 DRUGS AND HISTORY

Daybreak casts its glow over the prehistoric world. As the men hunt for food, the women gather plants, never knowing whether they'll find the "devil's poison" or the "flesh of the gods." But they are curious creatures, willing to try the strange fruit, the new berry, and the novel nut on the chance that it will stave off hunger.

One day the women come across a field of opium poppies. They sample a few, then pick the rest to share with their kin. The flowers' pods contain a milky white juice. Before long, the group discovers that these pods have more than just nutritional properties. Eating them makes them feel happy and relaxed.

Experts believe this is the way the first substance use unfolded, although they do not know exactly when it occurred. Scientists have dug up clues—analyzing fossilized opium seeds, human bones, soil samples, and

Early Winemaking

It's all in the pottery. Wine stored in clay pots leaves traces of yellowish residue. Archaeological chemists, who analyze this residue using sensitive instruments, have traced human wine-making back to the Neolithic Age (8500–4000 BCE).

The key ingredient in the residue? Calcium tartrate, a substance occurring only in grapes in large quantities. In a site dating back to 5000 BCE, archaeologists found not only clay jars, but also stoppers that fit on top. Early humans probably knew to seal their jars to prevent wine from turning to vinegar.

Later, around 2700 BCE, hieroglyphic scenes of grape-vines and arbors on jar stoppers show that winemaking in ancient Egypt had reached a high degree of sophistication. Wine jars were buried in tombs for use in the afterlife. An Egyptian wine cellar from around 2500 BCE contains the following inscription:

This is the wine-cellar.
The place for the produce of the vine is in it.
One is merry in it.
And the heart of him who goes forth from
it rejoices.

artifacts—to document the early use of psychoactive substances that altered psychological states.

In the high altitudes of South America, scientists have discovered that native people chewed on coca leaves from the shrub *Erythroxylon coca* for energy. Unlike other types of food, plants were portable and did not decay completely in those altitudes.

No corner of the world has ever been drug-free. Over the years, drugs have been used as medicine, in religious ceremonies, and for pleasure. Some foods double as drugs. Grains and fruits naturally ferment as yeast converts the sugar into carbon dioxide and alcohol, thus producing a body-altering drug.

The ancient texts of many civilizations—Sumerian, Indian, Greek, and Roman among them—are filled with references to drugs. In about 4000 BCE, the ancient Sumerians described opium, one of the oldest drugs, as the "joy plant." In about 2700 BCE, the Chinese described marijuana as the "liberator of sin."

In ancient Greece, wine was celebrated as a gift of the god Dionysus (or Bacchus in ancient Rome later on). The Greek poet Euripides wrote about wine in 405 BCE: "For filled with that good gift, suffering mankind forgets its grief."

Around the same time, the Greek historian Herodotus reported seeing the Scythians in what is now modern-day Iran throwing marijuana plants on heated stones and then inhaling the smoke. They had discovered that a plant used medicinally could also be enjoyed recreationally.

Because Native Americans did not have a written culture, they passed down legends rather than texts, describing the importance of mind-altering substances.

Shamans (the wise men or women) used psychoactive plants to enter what they believed to be a spirit world where they could receive guidance for the people.

Many social and cultural rituals protected early civilizations from the excessive use of substances. In ancient China and Egypt, for instance, people rarely drank alone, but as part of celebrations, such as the harvest. Native Americans used the hallucinogen peyote, a perception-altering drug, for rites of passage during the initiation of young people into adulthood.

In the Muslim world, however, religious teachings prohibited the use of alcohol. In the holy book the Koran, written in 651–652 CE, one passage states:

> Satan's plan is [but] to excite enmity and hatred between you, with intoxicants and gambling, and hinder you from the remembrance of Allah, and from prayer: will ye not then abstain?

By the year 1000 CE, trade and colonization had spread drugs across seas and continents. Arab traders brought opium to China on the Silk Route. Cannabis—later called marijuana—spread from China to the Middle East to Europe.

Alcohol was popular around the world because it killed bacteria, making it safer to drink than water. Most people back then would rather have risked being tipsy than dying of typhoid, cholera, or other diseases. The process of distillation, which made alcohol stronger, had been discovered by Arabs around 800 CE and brought to Europe by 1250 CE. The weak beer of medieval times gave way to more powerful distilled drinks such as whiskey. Other drugs—opium, for example—became stronger, too, as people found ways to isolate the active parts of the plant.

Tobacco in the New World

When Europeans set out to find a trading route to Asia, they accidentally found the New World instead. In 1493, Christopher Columbus brought back two items from the New World that would change the course of history: the pipe and tobacco. In his journal, Columbus described tobacco as: ". . . certain dried leaves, which gave off a distinct fragrance."

Not everyone welcomed Columbus's gifts from the New World. In 1633, the Muslim Sultan Murad IV of Turkey ordered that smokers be beheaded as faithless infidels. The following year, Czar Alexis of Russia decreed that smokers be whipped for the first offense and executed for the second. Such harsh punishments, though, failed to curb smoking. In England, rulers decided to tax tobacco to limit smoking. Drugs, such as tobacco and coffee, provided revenues for the royal coffers. In medieval Europe, public concern about recreational cannabis led governments to restrict the plant because its bulb contained a mind-altering substance. While the drug remained popular in India and the Middle East, farmers in colonial America grew the plant stalk, called hemp, commercially for making fabric and rope.

Opium in China

By the 1700s, use of the pipe had spread from Europe to China. This new method transformed opium from a medicinal herb people consumed by mouth to a highly addictive drug that they smoked. For opium users, the pipe's advantage was its speed in delivering intoxication. Inhaled opium produced a more rapid and intense effect than opium ingested by mouth. At first, though, opium smokers found the harsh, bitter smoke difficult to toler-

CHINESE OPIUM CONSUMPTION BEGAN WITH THE UPPER CLASSES BUT SOON
SPREAD TO THE LOWER CLASSES. EUROPEAN TRADING NATIONS FLOODED CHINA
WITH OPIUM FROM INDIA, WHICH MADE ITS WAY INTO OPIUM DENS.

ate. The Chinese partially solved this by producing
longer-handled pipes. Further refinement led to a water
pipe that filtered out the objectionable smoke. China's
growing number of opium addicts warmed to the new
innovations.

By the 1830s, opium addiction had become a major
social problem in China. Workers under the influence of
the drug grew listless and unproductive. The government tried to stem opium addiction by imposing taxes
and tariffs, without success. Enterprising criminals set
up their own black market for selling the drug illegally.

Most of China's opium came from India, a British colony, via British ships. In exchange, Britain imported Chinese tea to satisfy its tea-drinking population. Because the caffeine in tea is only mildly addictive, the English did not develop the dangerous drug addiction that the Chinese did with opium. With China's economy ailing and its people ravaged by addiction, the Chinese government took steps to restrict foreign trade. Finally, in 1832, the government tried to ban the opium trade. The British government reacted by declaring war. In the first Opium War (1839–1842), Britain forced China to continue to allow British trade in opium. The second Opium War (1856–1860) resulted in additional concessions from China.

Alcohol: The Devil's Drink

While opium addiction was taking root in China during the 1700s and 1800s, more potent alcoholic drinks, such as gin, had become popular in Europe. In London, gin houses advertised that one could get drunk for a pence and "dead drunk for two pence."

In colonial America, attitudes toward alcohol had varied. Some Puritan clergy denounced heavy drinking. However, many colonists considered alcohol necessary to good health. Long before coffee became popular, many Americans used alcohol as their morning pick-me-up. Alcohol is now known to be a depressant, not a stimulant. Colonists also used alcohol as a medium of exchange with Native Americans, getting them intoxicated so they would agree to unfavorable trading deals.

In 1784, Benjamin Rush, one of the pioneers of modern medicine, described the deadly effects of alcoholism as a disease rather than a human failing in his pivotal

Timeline: Development of Drugs

6400 BCE—Neolithic tribes make wine from fermented berries.

4000 BCE—Opium is called the "plant of joy" in Sumeria (modern-day Iraq). Wine- and beermaking takes place in Egypt and Sumeria.

3700 BCE—Native Americans in the Rio Grande area collect hallucinogenic peyote buttons.

3000 BCE—Coca chewing is practiced throughout South America.

2700 BCE—Cannabis is mentioned in Chinese directory of medicinal plants.

800 BCE—Greek writer Homer mentions use of opium to obtain relief from grief.

400 BCE—Greek historian Herodotus sees Scythians throwing cannabis on heated stones and inhaling the smoke.

625 CE—Mohammed orders followers to abstain from alcohol.

800—Arabs discover distillation of alcohol process.

1250—Distillation of alcohol process introduced to medieval Europe.

1493—Christopher Columbus returns to Spain from the New World, bringing tobacco and the pipe.

1604—King James I of England publishes *A Counterblast to Tobacco*.

1805—German pharmacist's assistant Friedrich Serturner separates morphine from opium.

1819—German chemist Friedrich Ferdinand Runge isolates caffeine from coffee.

1839–1842, 1856–1860—Opium Wars between Great Britain and China.

1848—Hypodermic syringe invented.

1859—German graduate student Albert Niemann isolates cocaine from coca leaves.

1887—Amphetamine synthesized in Germany.

1894—The Bayer Company introduces heroin.

1906—Federal Pure Food and Drug Act passed.

1909—The United States bans opium smoking.

1914—The United States Congress passes Harrison Narcotics Act, outlawing the sale of narcotics and stimulants, such as cocaine, without a prescription.

1920–1933—Prohibition (of alcohol) begins in the United States.

1933—Swiss chemist Albert Hofmann synthesizes the powerful hallucinogen LSD (lysergic acid diethylamide).

1937—Marijuana becomes illegal in the United States.

1967—LSD becomes illegal in United States.

1975—The Netherlands licenses sale of marijuana and hashish in coffee shops.

1980—West Coast motorcycle gangs create crystal meth (methamphetamine), a powerful amphetamine, using ephedrine from over-the-counter cold remedies.

mid–1980s—Crack cocaine and MDMA (Ecstasy) become popular new drugs.

1986—U.S. President Ronald Reagan signs the Anti-Drug Abuse Act of 1986.

1996–2005—Eleven states (Alaska, Arizona, California, Colorado, Hawaii, Maine, Nevada, Oregon, Rhode Island, Vermont, and Washington) legalize medical marijuana. The Supreme Court strikes down laws allowing medical marijuana work, *An Inquiry into the Effects of Ardent Sprits on the Human Mind and Body.* In it he argued that over time the consumption of distilled liquors, as opposed to wine and beer, could be addictive and lethal.

In the nineteenth century, a growing number of Americans spoke out about the social costs of alcohol abuse. Early feminists, such as suffragist Susan B. Anthony, believed that women bore most of the cost of their husbands' heavy drinking, because alcohol abuse fueled domestic violence and drove families into poverty. In 1874, suffragists founded the Women's Christian Temperance Union. As more people joined the movement, many states outlawed alcohol.

Morphine and Cocaine

With the Industrial Revolution in full gear, scientists embarked on a dizzying array of new drug-related discoveries. In 1805, a German pharmacist's assistant isolated morphine from opium. Morphine, which was about ten times stronger than opium, became a popular painkiller. In 1848, the hypodermic needle came into use. Eleven years later, a German graduate student extracted pure cocaine from coca leaves, opening the door to its medicinal and recreational use. (Such substances remained legal until the twentieth century.)

During the Civil War, soldiers received morphine to decrease the excruciating pain of amputations and other gruesome war injuries. Morphine addiction quickly became known as "soldier's disease." The new painkilling substances quickly found their way into hundreds of over-the-counter medications. These mixtures seemed like godsends compared to earlier remedies, such as the use of blood-sucking leeches. The natural painkiller in leeches' saliva had some limited use in pain relief.

Acceptable Uses of Drugs

It is hard to imagine today that drugs were completely unregulated in the 1800s. In England, Queen Victoria drank a special cannabis tea to relieve her menstrual discomfort. Other royals raved about a new wine, Vin Mariani, which contained an extract of coca leaves. Pope Leo XIII liked the wine so much that he awarded it a special Vatican Medal. The renowned psychoanalyst Sigmund Freud used cocaine to treat his own bout of depression. "You perceive an increase in self-control and possess more vitality and capacity for work," he wrote. However, after prescribing the drug to a close friend who ultimately died of cocaine poisoning, Freud regretted his earlier enthusiasm. Searching for a drug-free therapy, he developed psychoanalysis, the conversational method for treating emotional problems.

As some states passed laws banning alcohol in the 1880s, pharmacist John Pemberton created a new "temperance drink" that combined coca extract with kola nut extract. He called it Coca-Cola. Years later, in 1906, the manufacturer redeveloped the recipe without the coca ingredient.

Aspirin and Heroin

The Bayer Company, which already had introduced the aspirin, released a new, stronger painkiller in 1894. Bayer called it "heroin" for its "heroic" ability to fight pain.

At the time, experts saw heroin as an improvement over other painkillers such as morphine. In 1900, for instance, *The Boston Medical and Surgical Journal* reported: "It [heroin] possesses many advantages over morphine. . . . It is not hypnotic; and there is no danger of acquiring the habit."

Only gradually did the addictive nature of this and other drugs become clear.

A New Era of Drug Control

In the 1890s, new concerns about addiction arose around the world. Opium dens had spread across America, attracting not only Chinese immigrants but also musicians and writers such as Rudyard Kipling and Mark Twain. Since opium was legal at the time, an opium den was any building where the drug was sold and used. Opium smoking gave rise to the term "hip," meaning avant-garde, because users chose to lie in a reclining position "on the hip."

Meanwhile, sales of over-the-counter products for infants resulted in many deaths by overdose. In 1906, the Pure Food and Drug Act required manufacturers to list ingredients such as alcohol, opiates, cocaine, and cannabis on their bottles.

Around the same time, public opposition to the "filthy Oriental habit" led the United States to ban the smoking of opium in 1909. Concerns about opium also prompted international action. In 1911, a treaty signed at The Hague in the Netherlands required participants, the United States included, to limit the use of narcotics in their own countries. In 1914, the United States Congress passed the Harrison Narcotics Act, which outlawed the sale without a prescription of opiates and cocaine but not marijuana. Largely because of this act, the word "narcotic," long associated with the opiates, came to mean any illegal drug. In 1937, marijuana, too, became illegal in the United States.

The Harrison Narcotics Act ushered in a new era of drug control. Although not originally meant as a prohibition act, it essentially became one once it prohibited doctors from prescribing narcotics to addicts. Drug use then became a crime, not a medical matter.

Prohibition, an Age of Banned Alcohol

The outlawing of alcohol completely in the United States, which was called Prohibition, gained widespread support. Many reformers saw alcohol as the cause of numerous social problems of the twentieth century. Prohibition crusader J. Ellen Foster, for instance, declared:

> . . . the traffic in alcoholic beverages breeds disunion, overthrows justice, creates domestic strife, weakens the common defense, and fastens the chain of an ignoble slavery upon ourselves and our posterity.

Intoxication, reformers believed, led to destructive and violent acts as well as to an undisciplined and unproductive workforce. During World War I, reformers leading this temperance movement portrayed German beer as harmful to America's interests. This added a new economic urgency to Prohibition.

In 1919, the United States Congress ratified the Volstead Act, which prohibited the sale of alcohol, ushering in the era of Prohibition. The legal sale of alcohol gave way to "bootlegging," so named because smugglers hid liquor in their boots. Local taverns became "speakeasies" after a shopkeeper who sold liquor illegally asked her clients to "speak easy," or softly. In the 1920s, street gangs headed by notorious crime figures such as Al Capone and Lucky Luciano got into bootlegging because they saw it as more profitable than their old activities of prostitution and gambling.

During Prohibition, marijuana gained new popularity as an alternative to alcohol. Americans in the 1920s could buy "tea," as it was often called, for twenty-five cents or less, making it far more affordable than liquor. Recreational use of marijuana spread from Mexican immigrants to other segments of the population, including jazz musicians. By 1930, there were an estimated five hundred "tea pads" in New York alone. Authorities tolerated these marijuana clubs because patrons were orderly and the drug was legal.

Support for Prohibition, meanwhile, declined. In the late 1920s and early 1930s, a new middle class, many of whose members drank recreationally, rejected the idea of total abstinence. Many Americans also found the organized crime and corruption of Prohibition worse than the use of alcohol. In 1933, the United States Congress repealed Prohibition.

"Uppers," "Downers," and Designer Drugs

Drugmakers in every era developed new drugs. In the 1930s, amphetamines ("uppers") and barbiturates ("downers") came on the scene as prescription pills that lent themselves to recreational use. During World War II, when morphine was in short supply, scientists in Germany developed methadone, a synthetic opiate, as a painkiller. The drug would later be administered in liquid form as a medication for treating heroin addicts. By the 1950s, some people relished the idea of using drugs, such as amphetamines and barbiturates, to control the roller coaster of modern life. As one observer put it:

"Today you can take a pill to put you to sleep, wake you up, put on weight, take it off, pep you up, calm you down, boost your confidence, deaden pain."

In the sixties, marijuana became almost as popular as alcohol. Some young people smoked marijuana and a mind-altering drug LSD (lysergic acid diethylamide) as expressions of countercultural rebellion.

In the mid-1980s, designer drugs such as MDMA, a stimulant with hallucinogenic properties, commonly known as Ecstasy, emerged. It became popular at all-night dance parties, or "raves." Like other new drugs, it attracted users before researchers had a chance to discover its harmful effects. Also in the mid–1980s, cocaine gave rise to crack, a cheaper, more powerful form of the drug. Within a decade, cocaine moved from the wealthy who snorted it to the urban poor who smoked it.

More potent forms of heroin, clandestine drug labs producing methamphetamine, and Internet pharmacies followed. Internet pharmacies have since come under fire from federal authorities. Although physicians review questionnaires for medications such as prescription painkillers, consumers can provide false information more easily over the Internet than in a face-to-face meeting with a doctor. Federal authorities also have cracked down on the sale of the over-the-counter cold remedies used to make "home-cooked" methamphetamine. However, Mexican drug gangs are smuggling crystal meth into the United States.

As times change, so do drug choices. Drugs that were once illegal are now legal, and vice versa. In 1920—less than a hundred years ago—alcohol was illegal and marijuana legal in the United States. Drugs have been part of human society since the beginnings of time. They probably always will be.

OZZY OSBORNE PERFORMING WITH HIS BAND, BLACK SABBATH, AT A CONCERT IN 2005, HAS WRITTEN SONGS AND SPOKEN PUBLICLY ABOUT HIS STRUGGLES

2 DRUGS AND POP CULTURE

***Sex, drugs, and rock 'n' roll.* At first glance, it may** seem as if rock music glorifies drug use. After all, bands such as the Rolling Stones and Led Zeppelin are well-known for their drug use and their music. Some rock stars make no secret of living on the edge, of being rebels, and of breaking the rules.

Yet that's only part of the story. Neil Young's 1972 song "The Needle and the Damage Done" shows that certain rock songs do convey the negative consequences of drug abuse. While some rock stars relish their status as drug-taking rebels, others steer clear of chemical excess or have written cautionary tales about battling their own addictions.

Movies, television shows, and music videos similarly give mixed messages about drugs. The drugs that are legal—cigarettes and alcohol—often come across as a normal part of everyday life. In 1999, the United States government sponsored a study of movie rentals. Alcohol appeared in 93 percent of these movies, tobacco in 89 percent, and illicit drugs (mostly marijuana and cocaine) in 22 percent of them. Across all media, the most commonly portrayed substance was alcohol.

"The problem with many portrayals is that use of drugs is shown as fun and cool and has little consequence," said Donald Roberts, a professor at Stanford University. He coauthored a two-part study about substance use in the popular media for the White House Office of National Drug Control Policy (ONDCP).

Drugs and Creativity

For centuries, some artists have taken drugs to fuel creativity or to escape from the confines of the mainstream culture. Jazz trumpeter Louis Armstrong was partial to marijuana, which he called "tea."

> *"It makes you feel good, man. It relaxes you, makes you forget all the bad things that happen to a Negro. It makes you feel wanted, and when you're with another tea smoker, it makes you feel a special kinship."*

In the 1940s and 1950s, heroin took on new importance. The drug seemed to parallel the hipster mood of the times, helping users feel cool and detached. Singer Billie Holiday spent most of 1947 in prison for possession of heroin. In her famous autobiography *Lady Sings the Blues,* she advocated for the humane treatment of addicts:

> *People on drugs are sick people. . . . Imagine if the government chased sick people with diabetes, put a tax*

on insulin, and drove it into the black market, told doctors they couldn't treat them, and then caught them, prosecuted them for not paying their taxes, and then sent them to jail. If we did that, everyone would know we were crazy. Yet we do practically the same thing every day in the week to sick people hooked on drugs. The jails are full, and the problem is getting worse every day.

Rock in the Sixties

In 1963, Bob Dylan introduced the Beatles to marijuana. Musicians came together to experience the mind-altering affects of marijuana and LSD. Many songs from the countercultural sixties contain such prodrug references as "love grass," "trips," and "getting high."

Once, under the influence of LSD, John Lennon saw George Harrison's house as a submarine. The song "Yellow Submarine" was born. Although John Lennon denied that "Lucy in the Sky With Diamonds" was about an LSD trip, the song unquestionably shows how the simple love songs of yesteryear had given way to more improvisational works with colorful, descriptive phrases such as "tangerine trees" and "marmalade skies."

Yet during the height of the counterculture, some musicians composed negative songs about heroin and amphetamines. For instance, the band Canned Heat sang a song about "Amphetamine Annie" that includes the line "Speed kills."

The sixties culminated with the Woodstock Festival of August 1969, a three-day celebration of music and good vibes. But all was not peace and love. In 1970–1971, the rock world lost three of its brightest stars to drug overdoses: Jimi Hendrix, Janis Joplin, and Jim Morrison.

In the early 1970s, reggae emerged from Jamaica with its message promoting marijuana as the sacred herb. "Ganja," as it is called, is central to the Rastafarian faith, which embraces marijuana but shuns the consumption of alcohol, tobacco, and red meat. In his 1974 song "I Shot the Sheriff," Bob Marley describes the plight of a marijuana grower and his conflicts with the police. Marley portrays marijuana plants as living entities that the police are trying to kill.

The Darker Side of Drugs

With the rise of stadium rock and punk in the seventies decade, many musicians used a variety of substances, including cocaine, speed, alcohol, and heroin. Sid Vicious, the bass player for the Sex Pistols, died of a heroin overdose in 1979. The band Aerosmith fell apart for a while, partly because of the excessive drug use of Steven Tyler and Joe Perry. "We were drug addicts dabbling in music, rather than musicians dabbling in drugs," said guitarist Joe Perry of Aerosmith. People called Tyler and Perry the Toxic Twins. Finally, in 1986, they both gave up drugs and got clean.

Ozzy Osborne, too, got sober after years of drinking. His song "Demon Alcohol" runs counter to the spirit of songs such as Saxon's "Party 'til You Puke" that glorify heavy drinking. The rock and roll business has a long, ambivalent relationship with alcohol. Beer companies sponsor many rock concerts on the one hand. On the other, numerous artists have found alcohol to be the most damaging of all drugs. Both Bon Scott of AC/DC and John Bonham of Led Zeppelin died of alcohol-related causes.

The rise of crack cocaine in the mid-1980s brought a new flurry of antidrug songs. Positive songs such as Eric Clapton's "Cocaine" gave way to somber songs about the damage the drug was doing to inner-city neighborhoods. Donald D's "FBI (Freebase Institute)," for instance, describes children being neglected by their drug-using mother. In the song, the mother smokes crack with her friend while the children are left hungry.

Drug references in rap songs both glorify and condemn drugs—or describe the reality of drug abuse in the inner city. Rap references to illicit drugs and alcohol abound, but few can be categorized either as positive or negative. They're just a part of life portrayed in many rap songs.

The mid–1990s brought a new wave of rock 'n' roll deaths. Nirvana's Kurt Cobain, who was hooked on heroin, committed suicide. Overdose deaths followed: Blind Melon's Shannon Hoon, Smashing Pumpkins' Jonathan Melvoin, Sublime's Bradley Nowell. The National Academy of Recording Arts and Sciences (NARAS) launched a new drug treatment program.

Marijuana remains by far the most popular drug mentioned in song lyrics. Still, some musicians take a negative stance. In the Queers' song "Granola-Head," for instance, marijuana and hallucinogens come across as the drugs of people with nothing better to do with their time. The lyrics equate LSD use with being "screwed up."

Movies
Movies vary in their depictions of substances from the positive and glamorous to the negative and gritty. The

Anthony Kiedis, Red Hot Chili Peppers

Anthony Kiedis of the Red Hot Chili Peppers seemed like a rock 'n' roll casualty in the making. His use of heroin appeared to be out of control, subject to long binges, while that of his bandmate, guitarist Hillel Slovak, seemed more in check.

But, in a strange twist of fate, Kiedis lived and Slovak died. Trying to explain his friend's death, Kieidis wrote:

> He . . . had this hole in his soul that he didn't know how to fill. . . . He dealt with the pain that manifested because of that hole by using heroin. When he found heroin, that filled the hole. He thought he had found a valuable friend with heroin. What his sadness was, I'll never exactly know, but heroin diffused the sadness.

Kiedis's addiction almost cost him his career. After missing shows and falling asleep during practices, his band mates kicked him out of the Red Hot Chili Peppers. He got help, then relapsed, but went to recovery meetings sporadically. Kiedis brought Slovak to a meeting once but figured out that his old band mate wasn't interested in going back.

Kiedis tried to talk Slovak into getting clean for the sake of their music. Although the two stopped using heroin for their spring 1988 European tour, both resumed their drug use upon returning to Los Angeles. Slovak died on June 27, 1988, alone in his house. Kiedis wishes he had been there:

> If he wasn't so lonely and wasn't so into isolating—just being by himself, dwelling in the sadness of being so lonely—I would have been there or some girl would have been there or somebody else would have been there, and he wouldn't have died because it's not that hard to save somebody who OD'd on heroin. But he was alone except for his cat.

ANTHONY KIEDIS

At the age of twenty-six, Kiedis had lost his best friend. Unable to deal with his grief, he went on another heroin binge. Then he went back into rehab treatment. He realized how much his addiction had cost him. Staying clean after treatment hasn't been easy. Kiedis has relapsed, then gotten back on track. He's found other ways to "party." In 2004, he published his memoir, *Scar Tissue,* which chronicles his long history of drug use. His father, an actor who dealt drugs, introduced him to marijuana at the age of twelve.

In 2006, the Red Hot Chili Peppers released their album, *Stadium Arcadium,* bringing their unique blend of rock and funk to new heights of popularity. Critics praised the flamboyant Kiedis for his growth as a singer and songwriter.

"I have no interest in going back to the fear and confusion of my life during the last time I was using," Kiedis told *Spin* magazine. "I'm wearing life as a more loosely fitting garment, which fits me just fine."

1999 study *"Substance Use in Popular Movies and Music"* found that about half (49 percent) of the movies portrayed the negative short-term consequences of substance use and about 12 percent depicted long-term consequences. All movies showing illicit drug use received restricted ratings (PG-13 or R). Use of alcohol and tobacco were almost universal in movies.

Compared with pop songs, movies are more than twice as likely to link illicit drug use to negative consequences. The movies released in the 1990s and afterward portray drug use in a particularly dark light. The 2003 movie *Thirteen,* for example, paints a gritty portrait of the thrill-seeking behavior of young teenage girls in Los Angeles. The 1993 comedy *Dazed and Confused,* about high school students drinking, smoking marijuana, and driving around on the first day of school, is bleak, particularly compared with earlier movies, such as *Easy Rider* (1969), which showed drugs as a liberating force.

Television

In a recent episode of the hit show *The O.C.,* a character's marijuana smoking catches up to him. Seth has forgotten all about an appointment. His drug use makes him come across as silly and irresponsible.

According to the 2000 study "Substance Use in Popular Prime-Time Television" television programs differ from movies in several ways:

- 67 percent of television episodes with portrayals of illicit drug use mentioned some kind of negative consequence (e.g., loss of control, vomiting, loss of employment) while just 52 percent of movies failed to depict any consequence whatsoever.

■ 41 percent of television shows that referred to illicit drugs contained an anti-use statement but just 9 percent of movies did.

■ Tobacco appeared in approximately 22 percent of the television episodes compared with 89 percent of motion pictures.

Many of the drug-related story lines fall into two categories: sitcoms that mention drugs lightheartedly and dramas that cast them in a negative light. In an

AN EPISODE OF *THE O.C.* CALLED "THE POT STIRRER" IS AN EXAMPLE OF HOW TELEVISION SHOWS ARE MORE APT THAN MOVIES TO PORTRAY ANTIDRUG USE STATEMENTS AS WELL AS NEGATIVE CONSEQUENCES OF DRUG TAKING.

episode of *Law and Order,* for instance, a young methamphetamine addict who is accused of murder cannot remember anything and so confesses to homicides. It later turns out he didn't commit the murders but the experience in court has made him rethink his drug use.

Fictional characters on television consumed alcohol in 71 percent of all episodes analyzed in the 2000 study. Approximately 45 percent of the episodes that mentioned or portrayed characters consuming alcohol associated it with humor.

Cultural Messages

This Bud's for You. . . .It's Miller Time. . . . These slogans are broadcast so often, children can recite the jingles. Many of the ads convey the message that, if you want to get a date, all you need to do is drink.

Although cigarette companies are prohibited from advertising on television, they sponsor sports events and promote their products in magazines such as *Sports Illustrated, Cosmo,* and *Rolling Stone.*

Against this backdrop, antidrug and antismoking advertisements try to compete for attention. Increasingly, researchers point to alcohol and cigarettes as the true gateway drugs that precede the use of illegal dangerous drugs.

Responding to one study shows that underage drinkers and adult pathological drinkers consume between 37.5 percent and 48.8 percent of all alcohol sold in the United States, Dr. Joseph Califano, the former United States Secretary of Health, Education, and Welfare and president of the National Center on Addiction and Substance Abuse at Columbia University, said:

"It is reckless for our society to rely on an industry with such an enormous financial interest in alcohol consumption by children, teens, alcoholics, and alcohol abusers to curb such drinking. Self-regulation by the alcohol industry is a delusion that ensnares too many children and teens."

Meanwhile, the big cultural questions remain. Why are some people more vulnerable than others to the culture of instant gratification? When is it okay to show substance use as fun and enjoyable and when is it irresponsible? And, most important, how can the health of the public be protected against both the profit motives of the legal drug industries and the rebel cool of the illegal drug world?

In searching for answers based on his own experiences, Steven Tyler, the lead singer of Aerosmith, cautions against preaching or moralizing: "I'm a teenager at heart, and when someone says, 'Don't go in there,' that's the door I go in. You tell kids, 'Don't do it, just say no to drugs.' That's like saying, 'Cheer up' to a manic-depressive."

In 2004, the United States Bureau of Justice Statistics reported that almost one-third of high school students reported someone had offered, sold, or given them an illegal drug on school property in the previous year.

3 DRUGS AND RISK FACTORS

It is a common scenario. A group of teenagers is at a party, and someone offers the teens alcohol and marijuana. Not everyone accepts. Of those who do, some will drink and smoke marijuana only occasionally afterward. Others will go on to more regular use.

What accounts for these differences? This question has long perplexed researchers. Over the years, they have identified a complex set of individual, social, and environmental factors that make some people more susceptible than others to substance abuse. Instead of stopping at the experimental or recreational stage, they continue onto compulsive use.

Fifty percent of illegal drug use, including alcohol, begins between the ages of fifteen and eighteen. For some teens, drugs seem like a "rite of passage," a ticket to adulthood, a way to be "cool."

Those who start earlier are more apt to escalate their drug use. Figures from the 1999 and 2000 National Household Survey on Drug Abuse show that the highest prevalence of heroin, cocaine, and nonmedical prescription drug abuse over a lifetime occurs among the group that began using marijuana when they were fourteen years old or younger.

Of those who smoked marijuana when they were under fourteen, 62 percent went on to use cocaine. This tendency decreases as the age of initiation increases. Of those who began smoking marijuana after the age of twenty, 16.4 percent went on to try cocaine. For people who have never smoked marijuana, the figure drops to less than 1 percent.

Drug use runs in cycles, depending on the availability and perceived risks of the substances. When people view a substance as harmful, they're less apt to use it. Often drugs once viewed as harmful are reintroduced to a new generation. Researchers call this phenomenon "generational forgetting."

Amphetamine use, for example, tapered off after the "Speed Kills" campaign of the 1960s. Then, in the 1990s, the introduction of a new type of amphetamine, crystal meth, attracted new customers. Similarly, new drugs, such as Ecstasy, attract users before information is released about their potential risks.

As soon as some people get their first taste of a substance, they want more. "It feels good," someone says. Or "It lets me escape." These feelings, however, do not come out of a vacuum. Often, risk factors can be identified long before an individual encounters a drug.

Individual Drug Susceptibility

"I have an addictive personality," someone might say. While scientists are skeptical that such a personality type exists, many people believe that something about their psychological makeup makes it hard to do anything in moderation.

Depression and substance abuse often go together. About a third of people with depressive disorders have had a drug or alcohol problem at some point in their lives. Teens are particularly subject to feelings of depression and anxiety, partly as a result of the physiological changes of puberty. Certain behavioral characteristics such as impulsiveness, aggression, and the inability to delay gratification also increase the risk for addiction. Others turn to drugs as a form of "self-medication."

Lynn, for example, became part of a crowd of Ecstasy users whose members all had personal problems: "We were all broken in some way, feeling sad, hurt, and alone. Whether it was from a difficult childhood, a broken heart, or feelings of insecurity. We were a crowd of lost souls wanting so badly to be a part of something."

Family Patterns

Children with insecure attachments to their parents have a higher risk of developing substance abuse disorders than children with more secure attachments, researchers say. Abuse and neglect leave a lasting impact, making someone more susceptible to drug use as "self-medication." Often a parent's own substance abuse contributes to the negative environment, adding to the risk factors.

Chris Beckman knows all about the connection between family history and substance abuse. In his book *Clean, A New Generation in Recovery Speaks Out,* the former cast member of the MTV television show the *Real World* describes how his family's instability and history of alcoholism led to his own problems with drinking and drugs:

> *My story begins with the experience about half our generation has during childhood. When I was about three, my parents divorced. . . . Being a kid, I couldn't fully understand why my parents weren't together, where my father was, and what drove him to be around or not around. I couldn't tell the difference between who my father really was and what alcoholism drove him to do.*

Often Chris's father failed to show up for his scheduled visit. He was probably drinking, but Chris didn't know that. He just thought his father didn't want to be around him:

> *I remember Sundays looking out the front window into Trout Street, waiting for him to come, but he didn't keep his word. Often, all I'd ever see was the empty playground across the street. Over and over, after I had waited for what seemed like forever, my mother would walk in and say that Dad wasn't coming this time.*

Like many children of alcoholics, Chris saw heavy drinking as a normal part of life. Children of alcoholics and drug abusers are at a greater risk than others for developing substance abuse problems themselves. Many experts point to biological factors, saying that a predisposition toward drug dependency is passed down through the genes.

Environmental factors, too, come into play, as substance abuse changes the dynamics of the family. Children in such families are apt to witness numerous arguments and fights. Family life becomes chaotic. "I was too embarrassed to bring friends home," someone might say. If a parent loses a job due to substance abuse, the loss of income affects everyone in the household.

Teen substance abuse also can devastate families. Sometimes young people are introduced to substances through their older siblings. Other times they look on helplessly as a brother or sister self-destructs.

Sixteen-year-old Tina, for instance, posted an online message about her older brother, a twenty-year-old crystal methamphetamine addict. One day, her brother, already high from meth, came to see Tina and got into a fight with their stepfather. Tina called their biological father to come over, and he did, but then got into a fight with their mother. Her brother is now in jail on a robbery charge, but Tina hears that he owes money to dealers and plans to start up his drug use when he gets out: "I just sit there and take it until I am alone and cry myself to death. I have no one to talk to. My mom doesn't want to hear it, and my dad is never there. Meth doesn't just affect the user. It affects everyone around them."

Strong Family Relationships
Slogans such as "Parents: The Anti-Drug" are based on research showing that teenagers view upsetting their parent the main risk of drugs. Teens who regard their parents as being about as strict as other parents are approximately half the substance abuse risk as those who view their parents as either much more strict or much more lenient.

According to the National Center on Addiction and Substance Abuse at Columbia University (CASA), families with low risks of substance abuse share four characteristics:

- frequent family dinners (five to seven times in a typical week)
- low levels of tension and stress among family members
- parents who are very or fairly proud of them [their teens]
- a parent in whom they [the teens] can confide

Only about 26 percent of teens live in such households, however. In many families, teens hide the truth from or lie to their parents.

Peers

Many teens try drugs because they believe "everyone else is doing it." In fact, they aren't. Much depends on the particular group. Smoking marijuana, for instance, might be the norm for the "stoners" but not for everyone else. Groups attract members by projecting a certain image through their dress, musical taste, and behaviors.

Because "peer pressure" implies a lack of choice, some experts prefer the term "peer preference." Adolescents, they say, usually choose the groups to which they want to belong. Mindy, for instance, identified with the drug-using "rebels."

I idolized rockers and the hard-core lifestyle they lived, and I wanted to be a part of it. I would sneak out to parties on the weekends, and one thing led to another, and I tried my first line of meth. I was only fifteen at the time, and some kids offered it to me at a party. I was curious about drugs, so it was an easy sell.

The theories of "peer pressure" and "peer prefer-ence" are not mutually exclusive, however. Although voluntary, many groups exert pressure on members to conform. Sometimes groups change over time, and indi-viduals find themselves under more pressure to fit in. One popular athlete, for instance, suddenly found him-self shunned by most of his friends:

I had never lived with the fear that I had no friends, so I did almost anything to keep the two good friends I still had. One of the things I did was try pot for the first time. . . .I entered high school where smoking pot was "cool." I continued to smoke pot because that's what my new "cool" friends were into.

People of all ages—not just teens—look to their peers for acceptance. Because turning down an offer can be awkward, some teens prepare excuses to use ahead of time if confronted with a drug. Among them:

- "I can't! My mom checks me out the minute I walk in the door!"
- "I have asthma and can't smoke."
- "I have to go because I have a test tomorrow."

School

Availability is "the mother of use," researchers say. For more than ten years, the National Center on Addiction and Substance Abuse at Columbia University has sur-veyed teens and their parents about their views on the availability and use of substances.

In 2005, as in every year since the survey began in 1996, students reported that drugs were their number one concern (followed by social pressure, crime and vio-lence, and academic pressures). In addition, 62 percent of high school students and 28 percent of middle school students said they attended schools where drugs were used, kept, or sold. Students at such schools were three times more likely to try marijuana and three times more likely to get drunk in a typical month than those at drug-free schools.

Students who plan to attend college are less at risk of using illicit drugs than those who don't. Teachers and counselors, too, can be a protective influence. One teenager in Santa Barbara, California, for instance, recalls: "In seventh and eighth grade I got high all the time. When I hit ninth grade, I met a great counselor who helped me promise that I was not going to get high ever again, and I kept that promise to myself. . . . "

Poverty and Race

Although stories of celebrity addiction show that substance abuse transcends the boundaries of class, the highest prevalence of problems occurs in poverty-stricken areas. Why this link between poverty and substance abuse?

Experts offer a few reasons. First, they say, poverty weakens family and social bonds. Second, people outside the economic mainstream are more apt to ignore the expectations of society. And third, drugs may offer a temporary escape from a bleak life.

Substance abuse cuts across all races and ethnic groups. In affluent countries, cigarettes are sometimes regarded as a "drug for the poor." People on the margins of society also have high rates of alcoholism. Researchers estimate that one-half to three-quarters of homeless adults have co-existing alcohol, drug, and mental disorders.

Studies also shed light on the differences in use among ethnic and racial minority groups. Rates of alcohol and methamphetamine abuse are particularly high among Native American Indians who lead lives of poverty and despair on reservations.

Contrary to popular stereotypes, African-American youth do not have the highest rates of legal and illegal drug use. Whites and Hispanics do. In a survey of eighth graders, Hispanics reported the highest rates of drug use. Researchers point to early use as a possible explanation for their higher high school dropout rates.

In many inner-city neighborhoods, drug deals are a common occurrence, often part of gang activity. African Americans are more likely to be stopped, detained, and arraigned in disproportionate rates for illegal drug possession than whites.

The story of one Brooklyn drug dealer shows how the economic rewards of drug dealing can make it difficult to switch to the legitimate business sector: "I can't go up to somebody and say, 'Listen, I know how to buy and sell. I've been buying and selling drugs for years.' And I sure don't want to be no messenger, not after the money I'm used to."

Economic Costs

Not everyone with multiple risk factors develops a substance abuse disorder. Protective factors such as a sense of "connectedness" and involvement in sports can increase the resiliency of young people.

Programs that address risk factors aim to head off a costly problem. The economic cost of drug abuse in the United States is estimated at about $180.9 dollars a year,

Home Drug Testing

Before seventeen-year-old Rachael can go out at night, she needs to urinate into a cup. She's one of a growing number of teens whose parents have traded in the old-fashioned approach of rifling through their kids' bags and drawers in search of drugs for the more modern method of home drug testing. In the fall of 2005, Rachael was expelled for bringing a crack pipe to her high school.

Newsweek highlighted the rise of home drug testing in its April 10, 2006, article "My Mother the Narc." Hundreds of Web sites have sprouted up, touting home drug testing as a cheap, private, and effective method of monitoring teenage behavior. Simple urine tests, priced at fifteen to twenty-five dollars, show the results in minutes.

The White House Office of National Drug Control Policy has championed the controversial practice of random drug testing in high schools and middle schools. Many school officials, however, balk at the idea. They'd rather pass out pamphlets and hold meetings to let parents know about home drug-testing kits.

Not surprisingly, home drug testing has met with both praise and criticism. Supporters say the kits provide a socially acceptable way for teens to turn down drugs, letting them tell friends that they could lose their cell phones, cars, or other privileges if the results come back positive. Moreover, supporters say, the kits help deter use and detect a problem before it becomes too late.

Opponents, on the other hand, say drug testing can harm the relationship between parent and child, tearing at the bonds of trust. Drug testing, they say, is best left in the hands of medical professionals.

Sometimes the kits spark a drug war at home. Rather than suffer the embarrassment of urinating into a cup while his mother faced the bathroom wall, seventeen-year-old Matt admitted to his drug use. He said that he smoked marijuana only occasionally. He argued that since he was getting good grades, had been accepted to three universities, never smoked before school, and was not turning to other harder drugs, she shouldn't worry. Speaking about his mother's role, he says: "I've given a lot of thought to what she's supposed to do. It's really tough. I guess look the other way, but not approve of it. It strikes me that parents that are OK with it are not good people."

Rachael, meanwhile, has made peace with the drug tests. At first she tried to get other people's urine to pass the test. Then she decided to come clean. She had sold her mother's jewelry to get money for drugs and wanted to earn back her trust. Now when her mother and stepfather apologize, she says: "I tell them: 'You don't need to apologize. I know you're just doing it to help me.' And I'm glad that they did."

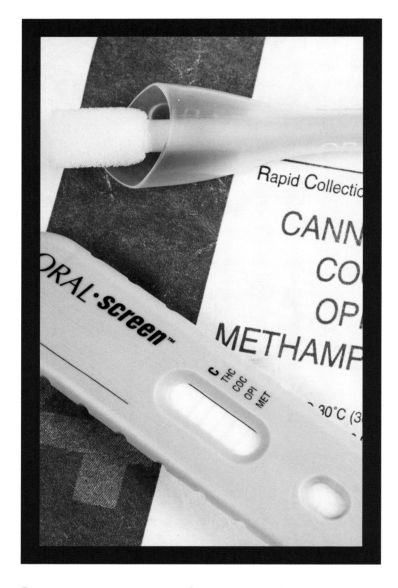

DRUG-TESTING KITS MEASURE A DRUG'S SMALL MOLECULES, CALLED METABO-LITES, WHICH MAY BE SHED INTO URINE, HAIR FOLLICLES, BLOOD, OR SWEAT EVEN AFTER THE EFFECTS OF A DRUG WEAR OFF.

which includes substance-related accidents, lost productivity, health care costs, and crime. These estimates, however, fail to take into account the impact of drug abuse on the quality of life of the family, neighbors, and victims of drug abusers, or on the drug abusers themselves. Such costs are immeasurable.

Two members of Florida Miami Drug-Free Youth speak to other teens about how to remain drug free in school and neighborhood environments where drugs are readily available.

4 DRUGS AND GENDER

Nicole smoked marijuana for the first time because she didn't want her new boyfriend Kevin to get the idea that she was a "dork." Although she didn't get high at first, she felt more mature and cool being around Kevin and his older friends. Then, in ninth grade, she got high at a party. Suddenly her shyness disappeared. She wanted that feeling to last forever.

Nicole is a good example of how gender affects substance use. Girls often use a substance to be sociable, improve mood, or relieve anxiety. Boys, on the other hand, are more likely to turn to substances to seek sensation.

Yet, despite their differences, the two genders have become increasingly similar in their rates of use. Although men generally use more substances than women do, the gender gap appears to be closing, particularly for teenagers. A report released in 2006 by the White House Office of National Drug Control Policy (ONDCP) and the magazine *Seventeen* found that teenage girls now match teenage boys in illicit drug and alcohol use. Girls surpass boys in cigarette and prescription drug use and are more likely than boys to start using marijuana, alcohol, and cigarettes.

Another study, the 2005 "Monitoring the Future" survey by the University of Michigan's Institute for Social Research, reported that, in eighth grade, females have higher rates than males for some drugs. As students grow older, boys develop somewhat higher rates of illicit drug use than girls (particularly higher rates of frequent use) and much higher rates of smokeless tobacco and steroid use.

Researchers say that young females have unique vulnerabilities for substance use. They're more apt than boys to be grappling with depression and/or the trauma of having been physically or sexually abused. Many young women also use substances to maintain their relationships with their male partners.

Because women have less fluid and more body fat than men, in general, substances affect them more quickly. Scientists call this phenomenon "telescoping." One alcoholic beverage has approximately the same effect on women as two drinks do on men. As a result, girls and women suffer from substance-related illnesses, such as cirrhosis of the liver, earlier than men.

Risky Sex and Violence

Because abused substances impair judgment, girls and women who use them are more likely to engage in risky sexual practices than those who don't. They are also more likely to be the victims of sexual assault. In a 2006 study by the University of Illinois in Chicago, almost 62 percent of sexual assaults were facilitated by the subject's own drug use while another 5 percent of victims were given classic "date rape" drugs. Other researchers have found that:

- More than one-third of sexually active teens and young adults aged fifteen to twenty-four report that alcohol or drug use has influenced a decision to do something sexual.

- Nearly one-quarter of sexually active teens and young adults age fifteen to twenty-four report having unprotected sex (not using a condom) because of alcohol or drug use. And 43 percent of teens and young adults—almost half—say that they are concerned that they might do more sexually than they had planned because they are drinking or using drugs.

- Two out of three AIDS cases in American women are associated with drug use. Even women who don't inject drugs are at high risk for AIDS if their partners do.

- Women with drug abuse problems experience two to four times higher rates of severe partner violence than nonabusing women.

Pregnancy and Child Rearing

Smoking cigarettes, drinking alcohol, and/or using illicit drugs can have a devastating effect on a developing fetus. Approximately 17 percent of pregnant women smoke, 9 percent drink, 3 to 5 percent are heavy or binge drinkers, and 3 percent use illicit drugs during pregnancy. While African-American women are less apt to smoke cigarettes during pregnancy, they are ten times more likely to report illicit drug use than white females, particularly the use of crack cocaine. Prevalence rates of AIDS are ten to fifteen times higher for African-American females than for white women.

Substance abuse during pregnancy raises a host of legal and ethical questions. How can society best meet its goal of having women deliver healthy babies? What can be done to prevent pregnant substance abusers from hiding their use or refusing treatment?

Boys and Steroids

Just as girls are catching up to boys in substance abuse, boys are catching up to girls in body image problems. Like girls, some boys are developing eating disorders such as anorexia nervosa or bulimia. In addition, boys are being treated for a new condition specific to males called "muscle dysmorphia," which involves thinking their muscles are not big enough. Many young men want to "bulk up."

When asked by researchers to choose a body type they thought would most appeal to women, young men singled out those with 30 pounds more of muscle than their own even though women in the study actually preferred a body type much less muscular. As a result:

- More than half of boys ages eleven to seventeen chose as their physical ideal an image possible to attain only by using steroids.
- 38 percent of men want bigger pectoral muscles.
- 45 percent of men are dissatisfied with their muscle tone.

Although some young women use steroids to boost athletic performance or increase their lean muscle mass, males have a much higher rate of use. Users don't get "high" in the way most drug addicts would recognize, but they get "pumped."

"I can understand the appeal of the look of power to a pimply-faced post-adolescent teenager," said Alan Klein, the author of *Little Big Men*. Anabolic steroids, which mimic the male hormone testosterone, also fuel aggression. Researchers call this phenomenon "roid rage."

Chris, a high school basketball player, went from a lanky 180 pounds to a hulking 220 pounds from anabolic steroids. His shoulders were so big, he could barely get on his backpack. When he'd walk down the hall, other students would say, "Don't mess with that kid." His personality changed along with his physique, becoming more aggressive and volatile. He got kicked off the basketball team for getting into fights.

After a friend who used steroids committed suicide, Chris threw away his vials and syringes. But as he soon discovered, quitting abruptly can lead to depression. He almost succumbed to suicide but, with his parents' help, began intensive therapy. He transferred to an alternative high school for students with emotional problems. "I could have had a scholarship to play ball in college," he said, clearly unhappy with how steroids had affected his life. "Basketball was my life. It's who I was."

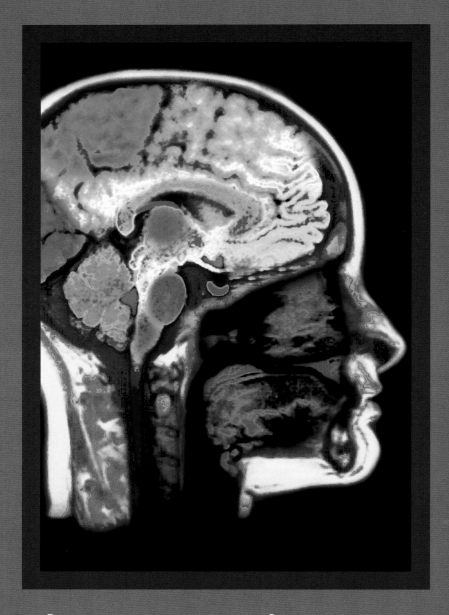

DRUG USE CHANGES THE WAY THE BRAIN WORKS. SMALL DRUG MOLECULES PENETRATE THE BLOOD-BRAIN BARRIER, MEANT TO KEEP OUT HARMFUL SUBSTANCES. HEAVY ALCOHOL USE INHIBITS THE FORMATION OF NEW MEMORIES IN THE DEVELOPING BRAINS OF TEENAGERS.

5 DRUGS AND THE BRAIN

Is drug abuse a "brain disease" or a personal choice?
Experts say it's a bit of both. In the beginning, people choose to use drugs. But once they do, prolonged drug use changes the way the brain functions. Habit-forming drugs hijack the brain's reward system, making it difficult for people to make rational choices.

The brain's reward system probably evolved to ensure our survival as a species. Drugs affect the same part of our brains that drive us to eat, mate, and fend off attackers in order to survive. When we do these things, our brains reward us with a sensation of pleasure.

In the 1950s, two Canadian scientists, James Olds and Peter Milner, discovered the reward center (also called the pleasure center) while conducting research on rats. The rats worked to get electrical stimulation in a part of the brain called the nucleus accumbens to the point of exhaustion in preference to water, food, or sex.

Some drugs negatively affect the production of important brain chemicals, such as dopamine. This naturally produced substance transmits nerve impulses in the brain, resulting in pleasurable sensations. Cocaine, methamphetamine, and heroin, for instance, quickly and extensively impact the amount of dopamine produced, giving users an intense and immediate high. Alcohol and marijuana, on the other hand, produce milder highs. LSD and hallucinogenic tablets called "mushrooms" appear to operate outside the reward system, making them more of a perception experience.

The more quickly a drug reaches the brain, the more dramatic its effect. A drug that is swallowed takes 20 to 30 minutes to reach the brain. When a drug is swallowed, it needs to pass through the esophagus, stomach, small intestines, liver, and heart before it can finally reach the brain. Other routes of entry take less time. A smoked drug reaches the brain in less than 10 seconds. A drug gets to the brain in 15 to 30 seconds if the user injects it into a vein, and 3 to 5 minutes if the user snorts the drug.

The Brain As a Command Center

The human brain is like a highly complex switchboard system. The command center of the human body, it sends and receives messages that allow us to identify pain, coordinate movement, orchestrate airflow, and think complex thoughts. It weighs just 3 pounds but contains billions of cells that connect in trillions of possible ways.

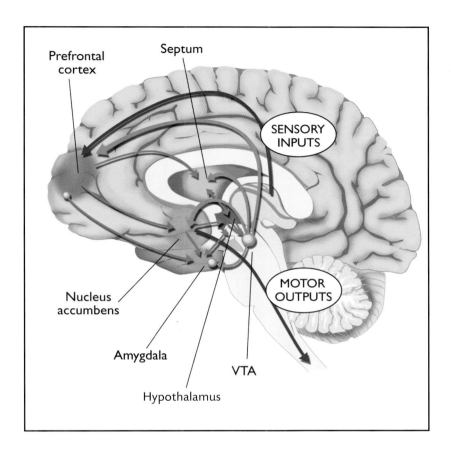

Prefrontal
cortex

Septum

SENSORY
INPUTS

Nucleus
accumbens

MOTOR
OUTPUTS

Amygdala

VTA

Hypothalamus

PATHWAYS OF THE BRAIN'S PLEASURE CIRCUIT

The brain is divided into three different levels—the brain stem, the midbrain, and the cortex—that correspond to our evolution as a species. The brain stem, which is the most primitive part of the brain, regulates basic bodily functions such as breathing and sleep. Located behind the brainstem is the cerebellum, another primitive part of the brain present in the earliest animals. The cerebellum coordinates muscle activity, balance, and vision.

Is Chocolate a Drug?

Many people call themselves "chocoholics." But is chocolate really a drug? No, at least not in a physiological sense, researchers say. Even though chocolate contains roughly thirty chemicals, the amounts are too small to have any noticeable effect.

Some people wonder if chocolate can make us feel "stoned," since it contains anandamide, a chemical similar to one of the active ingredients in marijuana. Probably not, answers Dr. Gail Saltz of New York Presbyterian Hospital. "You'd probably have to eat some substantial portion of your body weight in chocolate to approximate the effects of a joint," she says.

Chocolate also contains phenlethylamine, the so-called "love chemical" or "chocolate amphetamine." This, too, is in too small an amount to have any noticeable effect on the brain. The same holds true for caffeine, an ingredient in ample supply on supermarket shelves.

Not all chocolate eating results in pleasure. Researchers have found that people who overeat chocolate feel guilty and/or distressed. In one study, self-professed chocoholics were required to eat squares of chocolate even after they wanted to stop. The experience of eating chocolate went from being enjoyable to unpleasant. The PET scans showed different parts of the brain involved when the chocolate was pleasurable than when it was aversive.

More women than men report craving chocolate. Cravings are particularly high among premenstrual women, which scientists attribute partly to chocolate's rich magnesium content. Some people even regard chocolate as an aphrodisiac.

"The sensual experience of eating chocolate is very pleasant," says Dr. Saltz. "You might emotionally suffer if you don't eat the chocolate, but you're not going through physical withdrawal."

Above the brainstem is the midbrain, an area greatly affected by drug use. Sometimes called the "reptilian brain," it has parts that deal with emotions (the limbic system), memory (hippocampus), and the sense of reward (nucleus accumbens). The chemical messenger dopamine is synthesized in the ventral tegmental area (VTA), which sits at the top of the brainstem. The VTA sends dopamine to the nucleus accumbens, resulting in pleasurable sensations.

The midbrain controls the basic functions of survival, including the "fight or flight" response. When escape seems hopeless, some animals feign death. This sense of disassociation is common in humans who have been abused or neglected, putting them at greater risk of developing substance abuse disorders. The midbrain confuses the drive to use drugs with the drive to survive.

At the top of the head is the cortex, the highest and most developed part of the brain. The cortex distinguishes humans from the lower animals. It allows us to use language, reasoning, planning, and judgment. The dopamine reward system extends from the midbrain into the frontal cortex. As a result, a craving for pleasure and reward overwhelms insightful judgment and rational behavior.

Neurons and Neurotransmitters
Whereas a telephone system transmits messages across an electrical wire, the brain sends its electrical impulses across billions of nerve cells called neurons. A typical neuron looks like a tree, with roots (dendrites), a cell body, a long trunk (axon), and a spray of branches (axon terminals). Each neuron has as many as a thousand threadlike

branches that reach out to other neurons. When we learn something new, the brain builds more axons and dendrites, just as a tree grows branches and roots.

Communication occurs when the sending neuron transmits an electrical impulse along its axon. When the message reaches the end of the axon, a special chemical called a neurotransmitter allows it to travel over a tiny gap (called the synapse) to the receiving neuron.

Brain experts usually divide neurons into two types: excitatory and inhibitory. In general, excitatory neurons release neurotransmitters that stimulate other neurons while inhibitory neurons have the opposite effect. Drugs that affect excitatory neurotransmitters are called "stimulants," while those that involve inhibitory neurotransmitters are called "depressants." Most hallucinogens impact excitatory neurotransmitters.

Psychoactive drugs work in several ways to increase the flow of neurotransmitters. Some, such as heroin, resemble natural neurotransmitters closely and can mimic them. Others, such as cocaine, block the reabsorption of neurotransmitters so that they linger in the synapse. Common neurotransmitters and some of their functions involved in psychoactive drugs include:

- dopamine, which is a messenger for pleasure. It also affects purposeful movement. A loss of dopamine neurons, as in Parkinson's disease or long-term abuse of certain drugs, causes shaky, stumbling movements.
- endorphins, which are the body's natural heroin, an inhibitory neurotransmitter. They are released during heavy exercise (e.g., a runner's "high"). Endorphins moderate pain, promote pleasure, and manage reactions to stress.

- epinephrine, which is an excitatory neurotransmitter that prepares the body for "fight or flight." People seek drugs that mimic epinephrine, such as amphetamines, to stay awake, to lose weight, or to feel physically and emotionally stimulated.
- GABA (gamma-aminobutyric acid), which is a neurotransmitter that slows down brain function when depressants—alcohol and illegal drugs such as GHB, for example—are consumed.
- serotonin, which is an excitatory neurotransmitter involved in mood. It affects the visual centers of the brain, which become hyperactive as a result of hallucinogenic drugs.

When a neurotransmitter reaches the receiving neuron, it fits into a highly specific "receptor site" on the dendrite like a key fits into a lock. The whole process of neurotransmission takes place very quickly. A neuron can send an electrical signal and reset itself so it's ready to receive the next signal up to four hundred times a second.

The brain has its own recycling system. Once a message is processed, the neurotransmitter is either broken down by an enzyme or picked up by a transmitter molecule and carried back to the sending neuron for reuse at a later time.

Down Regulation and Tolerance

Neurons are constantly regulating their production of neurotransmitters. If the circuit is overstimulated, the receptors are downgraded so that fewer and weaker signals get through. The brain responds to a flood of dopamine by reducing the number of dopamine receptors. This process is called down regulation.

Without a dose of the drug, dopamine levels in the drug abuser's brain drop. Larger doses of the drug are needed to create the same initial effect. This is known as tolerance. Once tolerance sets in, the abuser needs drugs just to bring dopamine levels up to normal. Discontinuing the drug may result in withdrawal symptoms. The psychological and physiological symptoms of withdrawal depend on the drug.

Some drugs, such as marijuana, cause only mild effects when discontinued. However, others, such as opiates and alcohol, result in severe withdrawal symptoms. With opiate withdrawal, users commonly get goose bumps that resemble the skin of an uncooked turkey. Hence the term "cold turkey."

Many experts regard drug dependence as a "brain disease." The American Psychiatric Association uses the diagnosis of "substance dependence" to define addiction. Substance dependence occurs when a person has little control over habitual use of a drug that has caused serious negative consequences.

Whether or not the disease model helps or hurts, recovery remains a matter of debate. Supporters of the disease model say that people need to admit that their affliction is more powerful than they are in order to take responsibility for their own recovery. Critics, though, contend that the disease model perpetuates the notion that addicts are helpless victims.

PUBLIC ANTIDRUG DEMONSTRATIONS CALL ATTENTION TO THE SOCIAL COSTS OF DRUG ABUSE IN NEIGHBORHOODS, SCHOOLS, TOWNS, AND CITIES. PUBLIC AWARENESS AFFECTS ANTIDRUG BUDGETS AND LAW ENFORCEMENT.

6 DRUGS AND THE LAW

Few topics spark more heated debate than drugs and the law. On the one hand, supporters of tough drug laws argue that drugs harm not only users but also society as a whole. Illegal drugs, they say, promote crime and violence as well as health problems such as fatal overdose and HIV. They maintain that harsh laws deter involvement with illegal drugs.

On the other hand, critics of drug prohibition contend that it has been a failure. Tough drug laws, they say, have succeeded only in packing the prisons with drug users and drug lawbreakers. Like Prohibition (of alcohol), drug laws have created a black-market economy, thus attracting the interest of organized crime. Moreover, if the government regulated drugs, it could control their quality and so make them safer.

In the middle, a growing number of people recommend treatment over punishment. Drug courts, for instance, provide court-mandated treatment as an alternative to prison.

The "War on Drugs"

In the tumultuous days of the late 1960s, presidential candidate Richard Nixon called for a "war on drugs." He believed something needed to be done to curtail the rise of drugs stemming from the counterculture and social unrest. Having little patience for the complexity of the problem, he declared: "The country should stop looking for root causes of crime and put its money instead into increasing the number of police. Immediate and decisive force must be the first response."

In 1970, Congress responded to Nixon's call for action by passing the Controlled Substances Act (CSA), the first comprehensive narcotics control law since 1914. The CSA classifies illegal drugs into five schedules based on a drug's potential for abuse, likelihood of dependence, and currently accepted medical use. Penalties are harshest for Schedule I drugs and decline until Schedule V. The CSA classifies marijuana as a Schedule I substance.

While the federal law applies to all states, states also have their own drug laws, which vary widely. In the 1970s, the eleven states of Alaska, California, Colorado, Maine, Minnesota, Mississippi, Nebraska, New York, North Carolina, Ohio, and Oregon decriminalized possession of marijuana, eliminating prison terms for small amounts of the drug. However, some states implemented tougher laws against marijuana, such as "three strikes" laws where someone found in possession of any amount of marijuana received mandatory long and severe prison sentences. Other federal drug laws followed the Controlled Substances Act. In 1986, for instance, Congress passed a law requiring mandatory minimum sentences for drug offenses. States also vary in their views on workplace drug testing and mandatory sentences. Some state laws have longer mandatory prison sentences for drug offenders than for those who commit serious assaults or rape.

In the 1990s, several states passed initiatives permitting the use of marijuana for medical purposes. The United States Supreme Court struck down these laws.

At the international level, meanwhile, nations have signed drug-control treaties and agreements monitored by the United Nations. Penalties for distributing drugs are stiffer than those for possession. But whether or not these laws are effective in curbing the drug trade depends on whom you ask.

A Profitable Business

Illegal drugs are undoubtedly a profitable business. World trade in black-market illegal drugs generates an estimated $400 billion a year, according to a United Nations report. This represents about 8 percent of the total global economy—more than the international trade in iron, steel, and motor vehicles.

Because the drug trade is so lucrative, organized crime in many countries heads up the business, sometimes with the assistance of corrupt police. Terrorist groups often use drug trafficking to fund their primary activities.

Drugs arrive in the United States from a variety of sources. Much of the cocaine comes from South America; heroin from Southwest and Southeast Asia,

Central America, and Colombia; and marijuana and many other drugs from Mexico, Colombia, and Jamaica. The United States provides aid to a variety of countries for the destruction of illicit crops, alternative development, and other antidrug measures. However, the profitability of the illegal drug business makes it a formidable opponent. In Afghanistan, a farmer can make a hundred times more money from selling opium poppies than fruits and vegetables.

Once drugs are processed, they are most often smuggled as freight or disguised as other products. Drug distributors have hidden drugs inside children's electronic games, computer parts, decorative rocks, cans of soup, and hollowed-out Bibles and gravestones. Finding drugs in the influx of imported goods can be like looking for a needle in a haystack.

For smaller quantities of drugs, couriers, called "mules," hide the substances in their own bodies. "Body packing," as it is called, involves wrapping drugs in balloons or condoms, which are then swallowed. When the journey is complete, the drug mule retrieves the packets by defecating. A drug mule from South America can earn as much money in a single trip to the United States as in a lifetime of legitimate wages. But body packing carries severe hazards. If the package breaks open inside the body, the mule can suffer a fatal overdose. Mules are considered expendable, as they are involved in only a tiny portion of the business. Drug kingpins preside over increasingly sophisticated operations. They "launder" money through elaborate financial dealings to hide their activities from authorities.

Some analysts compare waging a war on drug trafficking to punching a pillow. When the pillow goes down in one place, it pops up in another. A crackdown on cocaine, for instance, might mean new business for suppliers of methamphetamine. Many experts say that as long as there's a strong demand for illegal drugs, new supplies will spring up to meet that demand.

Marijuana grows easily, making it a major cash crop. Some marijuana growers have moved their plants indoors to hide from authorities, but law enforcement planes flying overhead can detect the artificial lighting used in cannabis greenhouses. Law enforcement officials also are taking steps to curb the sale of ingredients used in methamphetamine. Thousands of illicit pharmacies,

THIS 2004 DRUG BUST IN TEXAS SHOWS THE EQUIPMENT AND TOXIC CHEMICALS USED TO MAKE METHAMPHETAMINE IN A SECRET AT-HOME LAB. IN THE UNITED STATES, CLANDESTINE LABS PRODUCE DRUGS SUCH AS LSD, PCP, AND METHAMPHETAMINE.

meanwhile, have sprung up on the Internet, presenting new challenges to authorities.

The United States spends about 66 percent of its drug enforcement budget on domestic and international law enforcement. The rest—about 34 percent—is divided between treatment, prevention, and research. Many critics of the nation's drug policy believe these figures should be reversed.

Drugs and Crime

Drugs and crime connect in three basic ways: the illegality of the substances themselves, the behavioral effects of intoxication, and the drug users' urgent need for money to feed their habits.

First, the illegality of the drugs themselves makes anything connected with them a criminal activity. Because people involved in illegal behavior are unlikely to complain to the authorities, disputes over the price, quantity, and quality of drugs are all subject to settlement by force. The drug trade also contributes to crime by diverting inner-city youths away from school.

A typical inner-city drug operation employs a variety of people, including children and adolescents who are easily impressed by the money and status of neighborhood dealers. Young people are often used in the following positions:

- Lookouts keep an eye on the streets to warn the dealer about police, rival dealers, and gangs.
- Spotters direct buyers to an ideal location to make a purchase.
- Couriers carry drugs to delivery points.
- Young dealers sell drugs in small amounts to other adolescents.

- Enforcers, usually gang members, control areas and increase sales activity.

Intoxication and Crime

Drugs and crime often intersect when a user's intoxication weakens self-control and compromises judgment. While impaired, drug users are more likely to engage in law-breaking activities. Users of alcohol, cocaine, and methamphetamine may become more violent and aggressive, acting in ways that threaten family members and others around them. When state and federal prisoners were asked about the circumstances of their arrests, 24 percent said they were under the influence of illegal drugs (but not alcohol) at the time; 30 percent cited intoxication with alcohol alone; and 17 percent named drugs and alcohol together.

Often, minor brushes with the law involve motor vehicle violations. According to the Monitoring the Future survey, approximately one in six (15 percent) teens reported driving under the influence of marijuana, a number nearly equal to those who reported driving under the influence of alcohol (16 percent).

Sixteen-year-old Amanda, for example, used to make a game of hitting trash cans while driving stoned on marijuana. Finally, after one accident landed her in the emergency room, her parents checked her into rehab.

Looking back, Amanda says: "Driving while high seemed like no big deal to me. Sometimes, I thought I drove even better when I was stoned. I convinced myself that the drug made me drive slower and pay more attention. But, of course, I was always speeding—or barely moving."

People who are addicted to drugs need large amounts of quick cash in order to maintain their habits.

MOTHERS AGAINST DRUNK DRIVING (MADD) SPONSORS MANY SCHOOL EVENTS FEATURING YOUNG SPEAKERS WHO HAVE LOST A FRIEND OR FAMILY MEMBER TO DRUNK DRIVING. MADD AVOIDS THE TERM "CAR ACCIDENT," BELIEVING THAT DRIVING DRUNK IS NOT AN ACCIDENT BUT A DELIBERATE DECISION.

In one survey of convicted inmates, 29 percent of cocaine and crack users claimed to have committed their current offense in order to get money to buy drugs. Drug users also turn to crime because of their inability to hold down steady jobs.

Often, too, criminal activity precedes drug use, showing that the economic links can work both ways. Many crimes result from a variety of factors (personal, situational, cultural, and economic), so identifying whether or not they're "drug related" can be difficult.

Mandatory Minimums

When lawmakers heard about the cocaine overdose death of basketball player Len Bias on June 19, 1986, they decided to take action. The result? A new law calling for mandatory minimum sentences for drug offenders.

Supporters of the 1986 law praise it for standardizing sentences that had once varied widely from judge to judge. Mandatory minimums, they say, send a message that "serious crime will get you serious time." The regulations reward offenders who give authorities "substantial assistance."

Issues of Race

Critics of mandatory minimums charge that they unfairly target minorities. In particular, the regulations call for harsher penalties for crack, a drug used mainly by blacks and other minorities, than for cocaine powder, which is used more by whites.

Supporters of the stiff penalties for crack say that, because crack is stronger than cocaine powder, it is more often linked to crime and addiction. The law imposes a 100-to-1 ratio, meaning that a crack dealer's punishment is equal to that of someone selling one-hundred times as much cocaine powder. Four of every five drug prisoners are African American (56 percent) and Hispanic (23 percent), according to a report by The Sentencing Project.

In addition, the critics say, mandatory minimums unfairly penalize the minor players in the drug trade. The high-level players hire couriers—often poor young minority men and women—to risk carrying the drugs. Often, the "big fish" in the drug deal take advantage of the "substantial assistance" provision and inform on "little fish."

Consider the 1993 case of Clarence Aaron, a twenty-three-year-old student sentenced to three consecutive life terms without parole for conspiring to distribute crack cocaine. His friends and cousin informed on him in exchange for minimal or no sentences.

"Clarence got the most time because he refused to snitch," said Robert Clark, a defense attorney for Aaron who spoke about the case on PBS's *Frontline.* "He refused to be a rat for the government. . . . "

Prosecutors argue back that informants are necessary to protect communities from the harm caused by drugs. It's up to the jury to decide whether or not the informant is credible, they say.

"If you want to infiltrate a Boy Scout troop you'd use a Boy Scout," says Jim Boma, the Assistant U.S. Attorney in the Southern District of Florida. "If you want to infiltrate a drug ring, unfortunately, you go to informants."

Over the years, mandatory minimums have been modified to provide a "safety valve" for first-time offenders and individual discretion for judges. Still, the prison population has exploded, with more than half of it made up of drug offenders.

Lawmakers also have passed regulations denying federal financial aid to college students convicted of drug offenses. The American Civil Liberties Union contends that it is not fair for college students who are drug offenders to be automatically denied federal financial aid while nondrug offenders, from shoplifters to murderers, can receive the assistance.

Drug Courts

After drug offenders clogged the prisons, people began to look for new solutions. In 1989, Miami invented something that would soon become a model for the rest of the country: the drug court.

Although court-ordered treatment has long been a feature of the criminal justice system, drug courts provide a special structure for judges and prosecutors to monitor an offender's progress in treatment. More than 1,500 drug courts, including ones specifically for juveniles, have sprouted up across the United States.

Unlike a traditional courtroom, drug courts use a nonadversarial approach in which the defense attorney, prosecutor, and judge, together with the probation officer, substance abuse specialist, and educational and vocational experts work to keep the nonviolent drug offender focused on rehabilitation. Drug tests are commonly used to monitor progress, and participants might be required to be involved in school or work activities to "graduate."

Successful completion of drug court might result in the dismissal of charges and/or reduced sentences or penalties. Many youth are ordered to drug court as a condition of probation. Judges typically act as authority figures—strict but encouraging.

"You end up establishing a relationship when you see a defendant once a week," says Judge Leslie G. Leach of the Queens Treatment Center, one of thirteen drug courts in the city of New York.

A typical day in drug court might include a round of applause for each participant with a clean urine test. Successful compliance with an electronic monitoring program might result in the removal of an ankle bracelet. Someone who has failed a drug test or missed treatment, on the other hand, might be ordered to sit in the "penalty box" and watch drug court failures being handcuffed and led straight to jail. Penalties increase in severity with each misstep. Judges can order "flash incarceration" and longer and longer jail sentences.

Researchers, though, generally credit drug courts with positive results. A study of New York's drug court system found that the re-arrest rate among drug offenders who had completed a court-monitored treatment plan was 29 percent lower over three years than the rate for the same type of drug offenders who opted for prison time without treatment.

Drug courts also save taxpayers money. A drug court rehabilitation typically costs between $2,500 and $4,000 annually per offender while incarceration runs between $20,000 and $50,000 per person per year.

Not everyone, however, supports the rise of drug courts. Critics maintain that drug abusers are better served by the public health system than the criminal justice system. Supporters, on the other hand, point to statistics showing that substance abusers have a six-times better chance of sticking with treatment if they're monitored by the criminal justice system.

Legalization Arguments

Many people who argue for the legalization of drugs point to the lessons learned from Prohibition. Outlawing alcohol was a mistake, they say, because most people are able to drink responsibly. Drugs, too, can be used in moderation.

Furthermore, they contend that the war on drugs has compromised civil liberties by allowing measures such as student locker searches and drug tests. A free society, they say, requires that people have the liberty to control what they put into their own bodies.

Proponents of drug prohibition, on the other hand, point to the harm caused by drugs. If drugs were legalized, they say, they would become more available, which would increase their use and add to the problems already created by legal drugs. Alcohol abuse is responsible for more crime and violence—not to mention health problems, absenteeism, and accidents—than all of the illicit drugs combined.

Legalization differs from decriminalization in that it would allow the government to control the quality, potency, and access to drugs. Virtually all proponents for legalization, however, stop short of allowing its access to young people. Under decriminalization, personal use of illicit drugs would be either overlooked or subject to civil penalties such as fines. Many proponents of drug reform focus their arguments on marijuana.

DEPRESSED TEENS WHO TURN TO ILLEGAL DRUGS, SUCH AS ALCOHOL OR MARIJUANA, FOR RELIEF MAY ACTUALLY INCREASE THEIR DEPRESSIVE SYMPTOMS.

7 DRUGS AND TREATMENT

Ryan got caught with marijuana at a school with a "zero-tolerance" policy. The school gave him a choice: expulsion or treatment. He chose treatment. His parents settled on an out-of-state wilderness program.

For the first month, Ryan had to survive with one set of clothes, a bedroll, and a sheet of plastic. The group, which included mostly cocaine and heroin users, hiked during the day and cooked their meals over a fire. Some participants begged to leave, saying they'd prefer jail, where they'd at least get a cot and maybe a little television.

"If you asked to go to prison, they [the staff] wouldn't let you because they consider that getting off easy," Ryan said.

Despite the harsh conditions—or maybe because of them—the group bonded. After a month, Ryan earned his way out of primitive camping. He spent the next month in a canvas structure where he could take a sponge bath using water he heated in a coffee can. His parents could visit for the day.

For the final phase of the program, Ryan moved into a real building with showers. He got his clothes back. The group learned reasoning skills and other tools of recovery. He earned a visit home.

Ryan found the program a bit excessive for someone who abused marijuana, but he admits the experience changed him. The year before, he was flunking all his courses in public school. His parents sent him to an expensive boarding school and promised him a nice car if he did well. But Ryan continued to smoke pot every day. After treatment, Ryan stopped lying to his parents and limited his marijuana use to the weekends. He started getting As.

While Ryan appears to have benefited from the program, finding the right treatment for the person is no easy task. In the past few decades, hundreds of new wilderness programs and "boot camps" for troubled teenagers have sprouted up, generating controversy. Several young people have died from the harsh conditions. Although some adolescents benefit from a challenge, others come back angry and resentful as well as curious about the harder drugs used by their peers.

In her article "The Trouble With Tough Love" in the *Washington Post,* author Maia Szalavitz argues against a "tough love" approach to drug treatment:

> *As a former addict, who began using cocaine and heroin in late adolescence, I have never understood the logic of tough love. I took drugs compulsively because I hated myself, because I felt as if no one—not*

even my family—would love me if they really knew me. Drugs allowed me to blot out that depressive self-focus and socialize as though I thought I was okay. How could being "confronted" about my bad behavior help me with that?

Zero-tolerance policies are similarly controversial. On the one hand, supporters say they send a clear message to keep schools drug free. On the other hand, critics contend that zero-tolerance policies unfairly treat casual drug users as addicts.

The Number One Health Problem

Research shows that the use of alcohol, tobacco, and illicit drugs is the single most serious health problem in the United States. Of the two "legal" drugs (for adults, anyway), tobacco contributes to the deaths of about one out of three long-term smokers. Alcohol results in serious health and social consequences for one out of ten drinkers.

Illegal drugs cause health problems partly because of the lack of quality control. Sometimes a single drug dose can cause death or lifelong infection. Intravenous drug users who share needles run the risk of contacting a blood-borne disease such as HIV or Hepatitis C.

Alcohol and stimulant drugs can prompt aggressive behavior resulting in injury. Many long-term drug users are in chronic poor health because they lead unsettled lives, failing to get adequate sleep and nutrition. The most common long-term effect of illegal drugs is a loss of interest and motivation in life, a problem that affects not only the user, but also society at large. About 60 percent of the economic costs of drug abuse are related to crime.

Economic Costs

While families such as Ryan's can afford expensive board-ing schools and private recovery programs, others who depend on public services often encounter long waiting lists. Some families find help only through the criminal justice system. Debate has erupted over whether teenagers without serious drug problems are taking treat-ment spots away from addicts who most need the help.

To complicate matters, the overwhelming majority of drug users do not see themselves as actually needing treatment. Of the estimated 3.9 million individuals who needed but did not receive treatment in 2000, fewer than 10 percent reported thinking that they needed help, according to the White House Office of National Drug Control Policy. Adding to the problems, many insurance companies deny payment for long-term sub-stance abuse treatment, so funding falls on families, nonprofit organizations, and/or the public sector.

Although treatment might be expensive, it's less expensive than the alternatives: higher crime rates, imprisonment, employee absenteeism, and drug-related illnesses. According to a 2006 article in *Dollars* & *Sense,* every dollar spent on drug treatment programs saves seven dollars in other costs.

Because addicts buy much longer and more intensely than casual drug users, getting them into treatment can cripple the drug trade, according to a report by the RAND Corporation's Drug Policy Research Center. Addiction varies by drug: 23 percent for heroin, 17 per-cent for cocaine, and 9 percent for marijuana.

Many taxpayers, however, see drug treatment as a waste of money. Often, they overlook the treatment period, during which an estimated 80 percent of clients stay off drugs, according to a report by the RAND Corporation. In addition, an estimated 13 percent of heavy users stop or reduce heavy use, some permanently and others at least for a while, as a result of treatment.

Jonathan Caulkins, codirector of the RAND Drug Policy Research Center, explains: "There is understandable skepticism about spending taxpayer dollars on these programs when only a small fraction of drug users who get treatment manage to quit for good. But that is looking at the problem from the wrong end of the telescope."

Diagnosing a Substance Abuse Disorder

Often treatment begins with an order from the school, the court, or an employer. In other cases, families and friends arrange an "intervention" to get their loved one into treatment. Sometimes, too, drug users "hit bottom" and seek help on their own.

Next, a treatment professional assesses the individual to determine the appropriate level of care. The three diagnoses—"substance abuse," 'harmful use," and "substance dependence"—range in order from the least to the most severe. The final category is generally used synonymously with addiction.

Types of Treatment

Usually the more severe the diagnosis, the more likely an individual is to be referred to inpatient treatment such as a hospital or therapeutic community. Medications often play a role in recovery. Just as insulin normalizes the dysfunction of diabetes, methadone, a synthetic opiate, can be used to treat heroin addiction. Critics of methadone

Drug Test?

One questionnaire that has shown promise in identifying drug abuse is called CRAFFT. Its questions list six indicators—Car, Relax, Alone, Forget, Friend, Trouble—that point to adolescent drug use. Two positive answers flag a substance abuse problem. The questions to ask:

- Have you ever ridden in a car driven by someone (including yourself) who was high or had used alcohol or drugs?
- Do you ever use alcohol or drugs to relax, feel better about yourself, or fit in?
- Do you ever use alcohol or drugs when you are by yourself?
- Do you ever forget things you did while using alcohol or drugs?
- Do your family or friends ever tell you that you should cut down on your drinking or drug use?
- Have you ever gotten in trouble while using alcohol or drugs?

complain that it substitutes one drug for another, but supporters say it protects drug users from a life of crime and life-threatening disease. Alcoholics can take Antabuse, a drug that makes those who drink alcohol violently sick. Other medications help combat cravings. Antidepressants, such as Prozac and Zoloft, are also helpful in treating the causes and symptoms of drug abuse.

For adolescents, a new group of "recovery high schools" provide academic instruction in a therapeutic environment. At the Phoenix Academy in Westchester County, New York, for instance, the 2006 class valedictorian spoke about getting a second chance to excel academically: "I learned how to express myself—I learned how to ask questions. It used to be that when I didn't understand what was going on in school, it was easier to stay away and get high."

Many specialists emphasize the importance of family therapy in treatment. In a study reported in a 2001 issue of the *Journal of Drug and Alcohol Abuse,* researchers found that adolescents who received individual and family therapy showed greater improvement than those in other types of treatment.

Twelve-Step Programs

Self-help groups, such as Alcoholics Anonymous and its many offshoots (e.g., Alateen, Narcotics Anonymous, and Marijuana Anonymous), provide a vital source of support for many substance abusers. In his book *Clean: A New Generation in Recovery Speaks Out,* Chris Beckman describes how his years of alcohol and drug abuse kept him from developing important social skills. He started overeating his favorite cereal out of loneliness. Worried that he was developing a new addiction, he turned to his support group for help:

> In Twelve-Step groups, we often use the word HALT to help us. When we feel Hungry, Angry, Lonely, and/or Tired, we are vulnerable to compulsive behavior. So, if I find my day filled with obsessions about getting to the gym, shopping, or even eating cereal, then it's time to halt and check my HALT status. Without fail, I'll find that I am hungry, angry, lonely, tired, or some combination of all of them. That's my signal to let go of the obsession of the day and get the help that will really cure what ails me.

Recovery

Unlike a broken leg that can be set and easily mended, substance abuse is a chronic disease. Recovery is a bumpy process, often marked by relapse. Individuals who develop the skills of self-efficacy appear to have the best chance of recovery.

Many clients find the adjustment from inpatient or day treatment to regular daily life particularly difficult. It is a time of transition from the destructive and familiar to the positive but strange. Nicole needed to bid farewell to her old drug-using "friends" who were too high to help when she overdosed on GHB: "I'd gone from partying with groups of people every weekend to sitting home every night by myself, crying. It wasn't easy giving up my addiction, but it seemed nearly impossible to give up the lifestyle, the 'friends.' Once I stopped using, they wanted nothing to do with me."

Often, relapses occur when the memories of the good times overpower recollections of the bad times. When individuals in recovery relapse, their families and friends face a new set of questions: Can the individual learn from the relapse? Is safety an immediate problem? What—if anything—will help this time around?

Sometimes family members disagree about the best approach to take. One mother, for example, wrote about how her son's drug problems caused tensions with her husband:

The fear that lives in our house on a daily basis is suffocating. My husband has actually asked for a divorce because he just could not take it anymore. This disease either makes your family stronger or it tears it apart. My husband and I are still together, but he and

*Matt [the son] no longer talk. My husband has taken
the "tough love" approach. I, on the other hand, am
his mom, and I am just not ready to give up. I still see
a glimmer of a light at the end of the tunnel.*

HIV/AIDS and Needle Exchange

Michele grew up watching her father die from AIDS.
Like about one-third of all AIDS sufferers, he contracted
the HIV virus through intravenous drug use. Michele
became an advocate for needle exchange, saying: "I
remember my father hardly able to stand and with
lesions all over his body. . . .Needle exchange could have
given me a relationship I never had. I don't want another
child crying over their parent's grave."

About a quarter of health care costs of drug abuse in
the United States goes toward AIDS treatment. Studies
credit needle exchange with more than a 30 percent
drop in HIV among injecting drug users.

Needle exchange programs and nonprescription
sales of syringes are part of a controversial new
approach to treatment called "harm reduction."
Supporters of harm reduction favor practical measures
to reduce the dangers of use rather than to call for abstinence. The movement grew in response to the AIDS
epidemic, with proponents arguing that the virus pre-
sented a greater threat to health than drug use.

Noninjected drugs such as crack cocaine also contribute to the spread of AIDS when users trade sex for
money or when they engage in high-risk sexual behaviors while under the influence of drugs. One study found
crack smokers more than three times more likely to be
infected with HIV than nonsmokers.

A Four-Step Program

Some critics object to the heavy emphasis Alcoholics Anonymous places on a "higher power." Seven of its twelve steps refer to God or a spiritual power. Alternative programs with a nonspiritual focus include SMART Recovery (Self-Management and Recovery Training), which outlines its four steps:

- Enhance and maintain motivation to abstain.
- Cope with urges.
- Manage thoughts, feelings, and behaviors.
- Balance momentary and enduring satisfactions.

From its roots in AIDS prevention, harm reduction has spread to other fields of substance abuse treatment and education. At the Fenway Community Health Center in Boston, clinical social worker Will Halpin uses a harm reduction approach because clients find it less threatening: "Sometimes the idea of coming to a clinic for help is overwhelming or nerve-racking because people feel that they will have to commit to something that they aren't ready for yet. . . . We won't put any agendas on you, and force you into anything you aren't ready for yet. We'll meet you where you are."

Tim, a seventeen-year-old high school senior, was arrested for public drunkenness and ordered into counseling even though he didn't think he needed help. He told his counselor he wanted to continue drinking, which he did only on the weekends. In the course of his treatment, he agreed to keep a log. The log showed that he drank more than average. He told his counselor he enjoyed the way alcohol loosened him up with his friends. His counselor taught him that he could get the same positive effects from less alcohol, which would also reduce such negative side effects as hangover and sleepiness. Tim was receptive to the idea because he wanted to do well academically in college.

In the case of marijuana, some specialists argue that the biggest dangers come not from the drug itself but from the damage a criminal record can do to a young person's life. Supporters of decriminalization point to the Netherlands' system of allowing marijuana to be sold in government-licensed coffee shops as an example of harm reduction that protects users from exposure to hard drugs. Another suggestion is to offer marijuana as a spray or lozenge so users won't suffer the negative health effects from smoking it.

Other harm-reduction strategies include:

- "Designated drivers" to prevent driving while intoxicated.
- "Sin taxes" on cigarettes and alcohol to decrease sales.
- Outlawing indoor smoking in public spaces to reduce the impact of secondhand smoke.
- Dance Safe, a program that allows Ecstasy users at raves to test their pills for contamination.

Substance Abuse in the Workplace

Finding a job these days requires more than just top credentials. Increasingly, employers are also looking for a clean drug test. Yet some wonder whether it is fair for qualified candidates to be turned down simply on the basis of what they do in their spare time. While civil libertarians criticize drug testing as a violation of privacy, most people agree that workplaces should be drug free.

Intoxicated employees pose problems not only to themselves but also to coworkers and the general public. Employees who use substances are also more apt to call in sick, work less productively, and suffer more health problems than nonusers. Although alcohol is often used as a social lubricant in work-related "mixers," excessive drinking has long been a problem for employers.

Sometimes the threat of a job loss can be a powerful motivator for change. Many employers offer Employment Assistance Programs (EAPs) and workplace-based prevention strategies to help employees.

Not surprisingly, many job applicants and employees try to beat drug tests by drinking water or using special products to dilute their urine. These attempts usually fail. Similarly, excuses such as "I was at a party where everyone else was smoking pot, and I couldn't help inhaling it" or "I was sitting beside someone who was cutting cocaine" tend to fall on deaf ears. It is almost impossible to test positive because someone nearby used drugs.

How to Help a Friend

If you're worried that a friend has a problem with alcohol or other drugs, you might be able to help. Sometimes an honest opinion from a friend serves as a wake-up call for someone with a substance abuse problem. Here are some tips culled from experts about how to talk with a friend about your concerns:

- Wait until your friend is sober or straight. Make sure the timing is right.
- Talk about your feelings. Tell your friend that you're worried and miss the kind of friendship you used to share.

- Write a note if you think that would be easier than talking face-to-face.
- Recommend that your friend talk to a caring adult or attend a group such as Marijuana Anonymous. Offer to go along to show support.
- Don't accuse or argue. Never accuse your friend of being an alcoholic or a drug addict. Refrain from accusatory comments such as: "Everyone's disgusted with you." Use a caring and understanding tone of voice.
- Preface anything that might be construed as criticism with something positive about your friend. For example: "I think you're a great person, but since you've been smoking pot, it's hard to depend on you."
- Be prepared for denial and anger. Your friend may say that everything is fine. You may need to back off for now. Even if your friend seems to be completely ignoring you, you've planted the seed.
- Bring the matter to the attention of a parent or counselor. Don't think of it as "ratting out" a friend. You could be saving a life.
- Take care of yourself. Get help from other friends or trusted adults to deal with the way the situation is affecting you.

MANSFIELD MIDDLE SCHOOL

Being Smoke-Free
Starts in our Community!!

Don't Bug Us With Your Smoke!

DEMONSTRATIONS SUCH AS THIS ONE IN HARTFORD, CONNECTICUT, IN 2002
HAVE LED TO ANTISMOKING LEGISLATION RESULTING IN SMOKE-FREE PUBLIC
SPACES, WARNING LABELS ON CIGARETTE PACKS, AND AGE LIMITS PLACED ON

8 DRUGS AND PREVENTION

When students at a small high school in Seattle gathered for a required assembly on drinking, many expected another "just say no" lecture. "While you're doing that, I'm going to be daydreaming about the big party coming up Friday night," one girl told the facilitators. But, much to her surprise, the leaders steered clear of a hard-line and instead encouraged an open dialogue about the pros and cons of drinking.

Such programs are becoming increasingly common in response to reports that the old fear-based messages and scare tactics don't work. Students are bound to reject the message that any drug use is dangerous if they see other young people using substances with little or no consequence. Well-known programs such as Project DARE (Drug Abuse and Resistance Education), which uses police officers to teach children about the dangers

of drugs and the ways to resist them, have yielded dis-
appointing results.

The RAND Drug Policy Research Center has found
that successful prevention programs share certain quali-
ties. Rather than focusing on the long-term risks of drug
abuse, successful programs help students recognize the
multiple ways in which drugs affect them now—socially,
emotionally, and physically. They also challenge perceptions that everyone uses drugs when, in fact, most
students do not. Moreover, successful efforts help students identify and resist prodrug pressures.

In another study, "School-Based Drug Prevention:
What Kind of Drug Use Does It Prevent?" researchers
from RAND found that successful programs have more
of an effect on legal than illegal drugs. The chief benefit
was to cut tobacco and alcohol use. Jonathan Caulkins,
the lead researcher, concluded that the programs should
be promoted differently:

*While we commonly think of these antidrug programs
as targeted at street drugs, it turns out that most of
the benefits that society receives are due to the cuts in
the use of legal substances. Taking this work into con-
sideration, it may make more sense to view school-
based drug education programs as health promotion
efforts generally, or as investments in the human cap-
ital of the next generation of Americans, rather than
as purely anticrime initiatives.*

Some experts recommend modeling drug education
on sex education programs. Much as sex education programs offer fallback strategies to prevent unwanted
pregnancy, the spread of sexual disease, and sexual
exploitation, drug education could recommend absti-

nence but also provide practical information about harm reduction. While such a program might sound like a "tacit endorsement" of drug use, Ethan Nadelman, executive director of the Drug Policy Alliance, says it's not. "With sex education people assume that, 'Oh, my God, if we tell teenagers about condoms, they'll be having more sex.' In fact there's no evidence that I'm aware of to show that giving that type of harm reduction information ends up resulting in more engagement of the activity."

Unlike the authoritarian messages of old, new school-based media campaigns, such as "Be Under Your Own Influence," appeal to young people's natural desire to be independent. Other new approaches teach life skills or engage students in positive activities such as sports or community service.

As authors Pierre Mezinski and Melissa Daly explain, drugs are not the only dangers adolescents face in life: ". . . excess in anything is dangerous. As soon as you start to abuse anything—in other words, to do too much of it—that thing becomes harmful. This is true not only of alcohol and tobacco but also, for example, of eating french fries, watching television, playing computer games—even studying."

Steps to Curb Binge Drinking

On college campuses, a wave of deaths of twenty-one-year-old students has prompted concern and action. Many students see being able to drink legally as a rite of passage. Games that promote binge drinking, however, can result in death. In particular, the game of trying to down twenty-one shots of hard liquor on a student's twenty-first birthday has resulted in many cases of alcohol poisoning.

Binge drinking, which is defined as drinking more than four (for girls) or five (for boys) drinks in a row, depresses the central nervous system. Because alcohol irritates the stomach, many drinkers vomit. Some binge drinkers die after passing out and choking on their own vomit. Alcohol depresses nerves that control involuntary actions such as breathing and the gag reflex. The common practice of letting someone sober up by "sleeping it off" can be deadly.

At the University of Virginia, the college has developed a birthday card program to prevent students from playing drinking games such as "21 shots." Students get a card that reads, "Happy 21st Birthday! We encourage you to celebrate responsibly." Enclosed are a coupon to a local restaurant and a wallet-sized card with Blood Alcohol Concentration (BAC) information, effects of different BAC levels, responsible drinking tips, alcohol poisoning information, and emergency resource numbers.

Binge drinking affects not only the drinker. At schools with high binge-drinking rates, students suffer a variety of "secondary effects." Research shows that:

- 34 percent of nonbinge drinkers reported being assaulted or humiliated by binge drinkers.
- 13 percent reported being pushed, hit, or assaulted.
- 54 percent reported having to take care of a drunken student.
- 68 percent were interrupted while studying.
- 26 percent of women experienced an unwanted sexual advance.

Not surprisingly, many colleges provide substance-free dorms to protect students against substance abuse.

Some colleges also have increased financial support for student clubs and organizations that are substance free.

Facing the Future

As much as many people might dream of a world without drugs, few see one in the immediate future. Instead, they wonder what can be done to address the problems that lead people to substance abuse in the first place.

In her book *Dirty: A Search for Answers Inside America's Teenage Drug Epidemic,* author Meredith Maran reports that adolescent drug abusers share a common lack of hope:

> *When kids have a history of failure—in school, in rehab, in their parents' eyes, in their peers', in their own—they see only failure in their futures, if indeed they see futures for themselves at all. When kids feel hopeless, the prospect of staying sober can't compare with the instant gratification of getting high. If we want our kids to make choices that will benefit them (and all of us), we need to ensure that they experience and anticipate success in their lives early and often.*

It takes a village, she believes, to raise a child. To this end, she recommends that society invest in policies to help families, schools, and communities. All parents, she says, should have access to quality child care, housing, family friendly work policies, health care, and mental health services.

Schools, she writes, should be revamped so every school is a small school—no bigger than five hundred students—and every class is a small class of no more than twenty students. She also calls for schools to provide mentoring, career guidance, and community service options. Young people, she maintains, should know what they *can* as well as what they *cannot* do.

On the community level, she calls for free treatment programs that offer a variety of coordinated services. And, finally, the criminal justice system, she says, should stop sending disproportionate numbers of poor and minority young people to juvenile hall or prison.

A Less Punitive War on Drugs

A consensus appears to be developing for a less punitive war on drugs. In 2002, a national survey by Peter D. Hart Research Associates, Inc., for the Open Society Institute found that Americans believe prevention should be the number one priority of drug policy. They ranked prevention (37 percent) ahead of punishment (20 percent), enforcement (19 percent), and rehabilitation (17 percent).

Over the years, people's attitudes have changed from a "lock 'em up" strategy to an approach that addresses the causes of drug abuse. Respondents offered comments such as: "You go to jail, you get out. You're not solving the problem. By the time they get out, they've just learned more tricks from other criminals. They just come out worse."

In addition, the study found that:

- 65 percent of the public favor dealing with the roots of crime over strict sentencing (32 percent).
- 63 percent consider drug abuse a medical problem that should be dealt with through counseling and treatment rather than as a serious crime that should be handled mainly by the courts and prison system (31 percent).

■ 76 percent favor required mandatory treatment rather than prison for those convicted of drug possession, and 72 percent favor mandatory treatment and community service for those convicted of selling a small quantity of narcotics.

■ 75 percent favor reducing spending on prisons and instead spending the money on public schools and community development programs.

Other researchers point to the burgeoning field of neuroscience as a new frontier of possibilities. Perhaps one day scientists will create a new cure for addiction or an absolutely safe means of intoxication.

Meanwhile, the debate over drug policy continues. What can be done to end the disproportionate punishment of minorities for drug offenses? Are proposals such as Maran's financially feasible? And, perhaps most important, what's the best balance between enforcement, treatment, and prevention?

Most teenagers today know someone with a substance abuse problem. It could be a relative, a friend, or an acquaintance. It is easy to see the lack of hope in their eyes. It is harder to know how to provide it. Before long, you and your peers will be taking your places as the neuroscientists, treatment professionals, and policy makers of tomorrow. It will be up to you to provide new sources of hope.

GLOSSARY

alcohol—A central nervous system depressant produced by the action of yeast cells on carbohydrates in fruits and grains.

alcohol poisoning—A sometimes fatal condition in which a toxic amount of alcohol has been drunk, usually in a short amount of time.

amphetamine—A class of drugs that act as stimulants, also known as "speed."

cannabis—A mildly hallucinogenic hemp plant used to make marijuana and hashish.

date rape drug—Drugs, including GHB, Rohypnol, and Ketamine, slipped into a victim's drink to assist in a sexual assault.

depressant—A drug that slows down the body and mind.

dopamine—A brain chemical neurotransmitter linked to pleasure and movement.

down regulation—A physical process that reduces the number of dopamine receptors when the body is flooded with excess dopamine.

Ecstasy—MDMA (methylenedioxy-methamphetamine), a drug that combines amphetamine-like and hallucinogenic properties.

endorphins—Neurotransmitters that reduce the sensation of pain and affects emotions.

epinephrine—An excitatory neurotransmitter that prepares the body for "fight or flight."

GABA—A neurotransmitter that slows down brain function.

gateway drug—A drug, such as nicotine or alcohol, that precedes the use of other drugs.

GHB (gamma hydroxy butyrate)—A central nervous system depressant commonly used as a club drug.

hallucinogen—A drug that produces sensory experiences that seem real but are not.

heroin—A derivative of the opium poppy that causes sedation and euphoria.

inhalants—Substances, including common household products that produce chemical vapors, that can be inhaled.

intoxication—A state in which a person's normal capacity to act or reason is inhibited by alcohol or drugs.

LSD (lysergic acid diethylamide)—The best known of the hallucinogens, used almost exclusively in synthesized form.

marijuana—The Spanish name for cannabis, the world's most commonly used illegal drug.

methamphetamine—A synthetic stimulant sold in crystalline form as "crystal" or as powdered "crank" or "speed."

neurotransmitter—The chemical messenger emitted by nerve cells that triggers a response in neighboring cells.

nucleus accumbens—The "reward" or "pleasure" center of the brain involved in all addictive drugs.

psychoactive—Influencing the processes of the brain (thoughts, feelings, perceptions, emotions).

steroids—Synthetic hormones sometimes used to increase muscle size and strength.

stimulant—A drug that speeds up the body and mind.

tolerance—A condition in which a drug user needs increased amounts of a substance to produce the intoxication once obtained from smaller amounts.

withdrawal—The process of discontinuing use of a drug.

NOTES

Introduction
Sources for Gateway Drugs Sidebar, page 11

Marshall Cavendish, Drugs and Society series, "Drug Use, Life Patterns," p. 347.

Office of National Drug Control Police, "Girls and Drugs."

Margaret O. and John F. Setaro, *Drugs 101: An Overview for Teens,* p. 87.

p. 8, par. 2, Marshall Cavendish, Drugs and Society series, "Advertising," p. 656.

p. 8, par. 3, David Boyum and Mark A. R. Kleiman, "Breaking the Drug-Crime Link," *Public Interest,* p. 18.

p. 10, par. 3, Alliance on Underage Drinking, http://www. gdcada.org/conditions/aloud/factsheets/adpromot. htm

p. 10, par. 4, Marshall Cavendish, Drugs and Society series, "Peer Influence," p. 656.

p. 10, par. 5, Marshall Cavendish, Drugs and Society series, "Drug Use, Life Patterns," p. 347.

p. 11, par. 1, Office of National Drug Control Police, "Girls and Drugs."

Chapter 1
Sources for Early Winemaking Sidebar, page 16

p. 16, par. 1–4, Marty Roth, "Anacreon and Drink Poetry: Or the Art of Feeling Very, Very Good," p. 314.

Sources for Timeline Sidebar, pages 24–25

"Marijuana History and Timeline," http://www.concept420.com/marijuana_cannabis_history_timeline.html

"Medical Marijuana," http://www.drugwarfacts.org/medicalm.html

"Meth Epidemic Timeline," http://www.pbs.org/wgbh.pages/frontline/meth/etc/cron.html

"Opium Timeline," http://opioids.com/timeline

"Peyote Timeline," http://www.erowid.org/plants/peyote/petyote_timeline.php

"Random Knowledge About Drugs," *Esquire* (February 2004), pp. 30–31.

"Timeline: Drugs and Alcohol," *New Scientist* (September 2006), http://www.newscientist.com

p. 15, par. 1, Paul Gahlinger, *Illegal Drugs: A Complete Guide to Their History, Chemistry, Use, and Abuse,* p. 3.

p. 17, par. 4, Marshall Cavendish, Drugs and Society series, "Ancient World," p. 95.

p. 17, par. 5, Roth, p. 314.

p. 18, par. 4, Islam—The Modern Religion, "Any Wonder Why Islam Forbids Alcohol?" http://www.themodernreligion.com/alcohol.html

p. 19, par. 1, University of Dayton, "Tobacco Timeline," http://academic.udayton.edu/health/syllabi/tobacco/history2.htm

p. 21, par. 2, Harry Henderson, *Drug Abuse,* p. 6.

p. 25, par. 2, Henderson, Ibid., p. 13.

p. 26, par. 1, Henderson, Ibid., p. 10.

p. 26, par. 1, Gahlinger, *Illegal Drugs,* p. 27.

p. 26, par. 5, Gahlinger, Ibid., p. 58.

p. 27, par. 4, Richard F. Hamm, "Administration and Prison Suasion: Law Enforcement in the American Temperance Movement, 1880–1920," *Contemporary Drug Problems,* pp. 375–399.

p. 28, par. 2, *Frontline,* PBS: "Drug Wars," Oct. 9–10 http://www.pbs.org/wgbh/pages/frontline/shows/drugs/buyers/social-history.html

p. 28, par. 4, Henderson, p. 12.

Chapter 2

p. 32, par. 1, Office of Juvenile Justice and Delinquency Prevention, http://www.ncjrs.gov/txtfiles1/ojjdp/fs200117.txt

p. 32, par. 1, Lauren Phillips, http://www.stanforddaily.com/article/2000/1/19/fewer/DrugsOnTelevisionMediaContainsMoreDrugReferences

p. 32, par. 4, James Collier, *Louis Armstrong: An American Genius,* p. 221.

p. 33, par. 1, Harry Shapiro, *Waiting for the Man: The Story of Drugs and Popular Music,* p. 78.

p. 33, par. 2, John Markert, "Sing a Song of Drug Use-Abuse: Four Decades of Drug Lyrics in Popular Music—From the Sixties through the Nineties," *Sociological Inquiry,* p. 194.

p. 34, par. 2, Aerosmith with Stephen Davis, *Walk This Way: The Autobiography of Aerosmith,* p. 296.

p. 35, par. 1, Markert, "Sing a Song of Drug Use," p. 194.

p. 35, par. 4, Markert, p. 220.

p. 35, par. 5, White House Office of National Drug Control Policy, "Substance Use in Popular Movies and Music, http://www.mediacampaign.org/publications/movies/movie_partII.html

p. 38, par. 5, Office of National Drug Control Policy, "Substance Use in Popular Prime-Time Television," http://www.mediacampain.org/publications/primetime/televsion_summary.html

p. 40, par. 2, Ibid.

p. 40, par. 6, National Center on Addiction and Substance Abuse, "New Study in Archives of Pediatrics and Adolescent Medicine and CASA Report Reveal: Underage Drinkers, Alcoholics, and Alcohol Abusers Consume Between 37.5 and 48.8 Percent of Alcohol Sold," at Columbia University (CASA), http://www.casacolumbia.org/absolutenm/templates/PressReleases.aspx?articleide=437&zoneid=56b

Sources for Anthony Kiedis Sidebar, pages 36–37

p. 36, par. 1, David Dodd, *Playing It Straight: Personal Conversations on Recovery, Transformation, and Success,* p. 78.

p. 36, par. 3, Ibid., p. 89.

p. 36, par. 5, Ibid., p. 88.

p. 37, par. 3, Alan Light, "Out of Their Tree: Red Hot Chili Peppers," *Spin,* p. 81.

Chapter 3

Source for caption, p. 42, United States Bureau of Justice Statistics, http://www.ojp.usdoj.gov/bjs/dcf/du.htm

Sources for Home Drug Testing Sidebar, page 52

Raquel Rutledge, "Drug Wars Being Fought at Home," *Milwaukee Journal Sentinel,* http://www.jsonline.com

Sarah Childress, "My Mother the Narc," *Newsweek,* p. 56.
Rutledge, http://www.jsonline.com

p. 43, par. 3, Marshall Cavendish, Drugs and Society series, "Peer Influence," p. 656.

p. 44, par. 1, Marshall Cavendish, Drugs and Society series, "Drug Use, Life Patterns," p. 347.

p. 44, par. 2, Marshall Cavendish, Drugs and Society series, "Risk Factors," p. 762.

p. 44, par. 3, University of Michigan Institute for Social Research, "Monitoring the Future: National Results on Adolescent Drug Use, Overview of Key Findings, 2005," http://www.monitoringthe future.org/pubs/monographs/overiewws2005.pdf

p. 45, par. 2, Marshall Cavendish, Drugs and Society series, "Depression," p. 262.

p. 45, par. 3, The Partnership for a Drug-Free America, "Agony from Ecstasy," http://www.drugfree.org/Portal/Stories/I_Could_Never_ Get_High_Enough

p. 46, par. 2, Chris Beckman, *Clean: A New Generation in Recovery Speaks Out,* p. 8.

p. 46, par. 4, Ibid., p. 9.

p. 46, par. 5, Marshall Cavendish, Drugs and Society series, "Alcoholism," p. 69.

p. 47, par. 1, Marshall Cavendish Drugs and Society series, "Family Environment," p. 395.

p. 47, par. 3, Parents. The Anti-Drug, "My Big Brother Is a Meth Addict," http://www.theantidrug.com/community/ktopics.asp? topic=3

p. 48, par. 1, CASA, "National Survey of American Attitudes on Substance Abuse X: Teens and Parents." http://www.casacolumbia.org

p. 48 par. 2, Ibid.

p. 48, par. 4, Marshall Cavendish, Drugs and Society series, "Peer Influence," p. 657.

p. 48, par. 5, Partnership for a Drug-Free America, "I Could Never Get High Enough," http://www.drugfree.org/Portal/Stories/ I_Could_Never_Get_High_Enough

p. 49, par. 2, Marijuana Anonymous. www. marijuanaanonymous.org/ Pages/teens.html

p. 49, par. 4, Syndistar Inc. Educational Publishers, "The Refusal Challenge," http://www.intheknowzone.come/whattosay/testresults.asp

p. 49, par. 6, CASA, http://www.casacolumbia.org/Absolutenm/articlefiles/Teen_Survey_Report_2005

p. 49, par. 7, Ibid.

p. 49, par. 8, Ibid.

p. 50, par. 2, University of Michigan Institute for Social Research, http://www.monitoringthefuture.org/pubs/monographs/overview2005.pdf

p. 50, par. 2, The Partnership for a Drug-Free America, "My 17th Birthday," http://www.drugfree.org/Portal/Stories/My17th Birthday

p. 50, par. 4, Marshall Cavendish, Drugs and Society series, "Class and Drug Use," p. 180.

p. 50, par. 5, Ibid., p. 179.

p. 50, par. 5, Ibid., p. 694.

p. 51, par. 1, David Melmer, "Drug Abuse, Suicide Among Top Tribal Concerns," *Indian Country Toda,* http://www.msnbc.msn.com/id/12517348

p. 51, par. 1, University of Michigan Institute for Social Research, http://www.monitoringthefuture.org/pubs/monographs/overview2005.pdf

p. 51, par. 3, Marshall Cavendish, Drugs and Society series, "Race and Drugs," p. 732.

p. 51, par. 4, "Crime as Business: The Career of Drug Dealer in a Brooklyn Housing Project," http://www.children/smartlibrary.org/NewInterface/segment/cfm?segment=1709

p. 51, par. 6, White House Office of National Drug Control Policy, "The Economic Costs of Drug Abuse in the United States, 1992-2002," http://www.whitehousedrugpolicy.gov/publications/index.html

Chapter 4

p. 57, par. 1, Nicole O'Bryan with Cecilia Goodnow, "I Was Addicted to Crystal Meth," *CosmoGirl!,* p. 120.

p. 57, par. 2, Marshall Cavendish, Drugs and Society series, "Women and Drugs," p. 875.

p. 58, par. 1, White House Office of National Drug Control Policy, "Girls and Drugs," http://www.mediacampaign.org/newsroom/press06/020906.html

p. 58, par. 2, University of Michigan Institute for Social Research, http://www.monitoringthefuture.org/pubs/monographs/overview 2005.pdf

p. 58, par. 2, Marshall Cavendish, Drugs and Society series, "Women and Drugs," p. 875.

p. 58, par. 3, Ralph Nader, "Drug Abuse Needs to be Addressed Along Gender Lines," Knight Ridder/Tribune New Service, Feb. 21, 2003.

p. 59, par. 1, *Chicago Sun-Times,* "Most Sexual Assaults Involve Drugs," http://www.dpna.org/5sexualassaults.htm.

p. 59, par. 4, The National Campaign to Prevent Teen Pregnancy, "Sex and Drugs," http://www.teenpregnancy.org/resources/reading/fact_sheets/drugsondcp.asp

p. 59, par. 3, CASA, *Women Under the Influence,* p. 93.

p. 59, par. 4, Ibid., 94.

p. 60, par. 1, Marshall Cavendish, Drugs and Society series, "Race and Drugs," p. 733.

p. 60, par. 1, CASA, p. 129.

p. 60, par. 4, Drugstory, "Muscle Madness: The Ugly Connection Between Body Image and SteroidAbuse." http://www.drugstory.org/pdfs/musclemadness2.pdf

p. 60, par. 5, Ibid.

p. 61, par. 2, Andrew Taber, "Roid Rage," *Salon* (November 18, 1999). http://www.solon.com/health/feature/1999/11/18/steroids/index.htlml (Accessed Mary 23, 2006)

p. 61, par. 3, Jerry Adler, "Toxic Strength," *Newsweek,* p. 44.

p. 61, par. 4, Ibid.

Chapter 5

p. 64, par. 1, Drew Pinsky with Todd Gold. *Cracked: Putting Broken Lives Together Again—A Doctor's Story.* New York: HarperCollins Publishers, 2003, pp. 57–58, 186.

p. 64, par. 2, *Psychology Today* Staff, "Inside the Addict's Brain," http://www.psychologytoday.com/articles/pto-19940901-000022.html (Accessed July 16, 2006).

Sources for Is Chocolate a Drug? Page 66

Penny, "Cuckoo for Cocoa?" *New York* magazine, (November 1, 2004). Web site.

Northwestern University, "Measuring Brain Activity in People Eating Chocolate," www.nwu.edu

"Chocolate," http://www.chocolate.org (accessed June 13, 2006)

"Cuckoo for Cocoa?" *New York* magazine, November 1, 2004, http://newyorkmetro.com/nymetro/urban/strategist/everything/chocolate/10188/.

p. 68, par. 1, Paul Gahlinger, *Illegal Drugs: A Complete Guide to Their History, Chemistry, Use, and Abuse.* New York: Plume, 2004. pp. 29–130.

p. 68, par. 2, Gahlinger, 136.

p. 70, par. 1, National Institute on Drug Abuse, "The Brain & Addiction." http://teens.drugabuse.gov/facts/facts_brain2.asp (Accessed June 4, 2006).

p. 71, par. 4, "Addiction," Marshall Cavendish, Drugs and Society series, p. 26.

p. 71, par. 4, Tamara Roleff, ed., *Drug Abuse: Opposing Viewpoints.* Farmington Hill, MI: Greenhaven Press, 2005, p. 71, 85

Chapter 6

p. 74, par. 2, Henderson, *Drug Abuse,* p. 21.

p. 75, par. 4, Drug Policy Alliance, "Drug Treatment v. Supply Side Measures," http://www.drugpolicy.org/library/factsheets/drugtreatment/index.cfm

p. 76, par. 1, Margaret O. Hyde and John F. Setaro, M.D., *Drugs 101: An Overview for Teens,* p. 106.

p. 76, par. 2, Drug Policy Alliance, http://www.drugpolicy.org/library/factsheets/drugtreatment/index.cfm

p. 76, par. 3, Hyde and Setaro, p. 106.

p. 78, par. 2, Roleff, ed., *The War on Drugs,* p. 34.

p. 78, par. 6, Gahlinger, *Illegal Drugs,* p. 174.

p. 79, par. 2, Boyum and Kleiman, "Breaking the Drug-Crime Link," p. 18.

p. 79, par. 3, White House Office of National Drug Control Policy, "Teens, Drugs, and Driving: Steer Clear of Pot," http://www.mediacampaign.org/steerclear/factsheet.html

p. 79, par. 4, John DiConsiglio, "The High Road: Amanda Used to Smoke Marijuana and Then Drive a Car," p. 10.

p. 81, par. 1, Boyum and Kleiman, "Breaking the Drug-Crime Link," p.18.

p. 81, par. 4, Roleff, ed., p. 110.

p. 82, par. 1, Ryan King and Marc Mauer, "Distorted Priorities: Drug Offenders in State Prisons," http://www.sentencingproject.org

p. 82, par. 4, *Frontline,* "Snitch," Clark case, http://www.pbs.org/wgbh/pages/frontline/shows/snitch/cases/clark.html

p. 82, par. 6, *Frontline,* "Snitch," Boma case, pages/frontline/shows/snitch/case/ boma.html

p. 82, par. 7, Sterling and Stewart, "Undo the Legacy of Len Bias's Death," *Washington Post,* p. A21.

p. 83, par. 1, American Civil Liberties Union, "ACLU complaint, *SSDP v. Spellings,*" http://www.aclu.org/drugpolicy/gen/

p. 83, par. 4, White House Office of National Drug Control Policy, "Drug Courts," http://www.whitehousedrugpolicy/gov/enforce/drugcourt.html

p. 84, par. 2, Paul Von Zielbauer, "Court Treatment System Found to

Help Drug Offenders Stay Clean," http://www.nytimes.com

p. 84, par. 5, Marshall Cavendish Drugs and Society series, "Penalties and Punishment," p. 661.

p. 84, par. 6, United States Department of Justice, Office of Justice Programs, "Drug Courts: The Second Decade," http://www.ojp.usddoj.gov/nij

p. 84, par. 8, Boyum and Kleiman, "Breaking the Drug-Crime Link," p. 18.

Chapter 7

Source for SMART Recover Sidebar on p. 92

Zoler, "History Flags Teen Drug Abuse Better Than a Drug Test," *Family Practice News*, p. 34.

SMART Recovery, http://www.smartrecovery.org

p. 87, par. 1, Narconon Southern California, "Drug Rehab A Tough Lesson," http://www.addictionca.com/news-left.htm?aid=422

p. 88, par. 5, Szalavitz, "The Trouble with Tough Love," *Washington Post*, B01.

p. 89, par. 3, Office of Juvenile Justice and Delinquency Prevention, "Substance Abuse: The Nation's Number One Health Problem," OJJDP Fact Sheet, http://www.ncjrs.gov/txfiles1/ojjdp/fs200117.txt

p. 89, par. 5, Marshall Cavendish Drugs and Society series, "Advertising," p. 41.

p. 89, par. 6, White House Office of National Drug Control Policy, "The Economic Costs of Drug Abuse in the United States, 1992–2002," http://www.whitehousedrugpolicy.gov/publications/index.html

p. 89, par. 7, White House Office of National Dug Control Policy, "National Priorities II: Healing America's Drug Users, 2002," http://www.whitehousedrugpolicy.gov/publications/policy/03ndcs/2priorities.html

p. 90, par. 3, "The Short Run: Drug Treatment Pays for Itself Many Times Over," *Dollars and Sense,* http://www.dollarsandsense.org/blog/

p. 90, par. 4, RAND Drug Policy Research Center, "Assessing U.S. Drug Problems and Policy," 2005, http://www.rand.org

p. 90, par. 5, RAND Corporation. "Treatment: Effective (But Unpopular) Weapon Against Drugs," http://www.rand.org/ publications/randreview/issues/RRR.spring95.crime/treatment.html

p. 93, par. 1, Phoenix Academy, Westchester, NY, "Proud Phoenix Academy Students Face the Future. . . Drug-Free," http:// www.phoenixhouse.org/NewYoirk/WhatsNew/PressReleases/ FacetheFuture.html

p. 93, par. 4, Beckman, *Clean,* p. 127.

p. 94, par. 2, Nicole Hansen, The Partnership for a Drug-Free America, "Real Drugs, False Friends," http://www.drugfree.org. Teen/teen_1.htm.

p. 94, par. 5, Lauren Huston, "Our Continued Struggle," http:// www.drugfree.org/Portal/Stories/Our_Continued_Struggle

p. 95, par. 2, The Dogwood Center, "AIDS Survivors," http://www.dogwoodcenter.org/survivors/stories.html

p. 95, par. 3, Marshall Cavendish, Drugs and Society series, "Economic Costs of Addiction," p. 360.

p. 95, par. 3, Marshall Cavendish, Drugs and Society series, "Needle Exchange Programs," p. 594.

p. 95, par. 5, National Institute of Drug Abuse. "NIDA InfoFacts: Drug Abuse and AIDS," http://www.nida.nih.gov/Infofacts/ drugabuse.html

p. 96, par. 2, Fenway Community Health, "Personal Stories," http://www.fenwayhealth.org/site/PageServer?pagename=CM_ ps_personalstories

p. 96, par. 3, Craig Forte, LCSW, "A Harm Reduction Approach to Treating Problem Adolescent Alcohol Use," Clinical Social Work Society, http://www.clinicalsocialworksoety.org/documents/ HarmReductionApproach.doc

Chapter 8

p. 101, par. 1, G. Alan Marlatt, Ph.D., "Harm Reduction Works," *Alcohol Problems & Solutions,* http://www2.Potsdam.edu/hansondj /YouthIssues/104634958.html

p. 102, par. 2, RAND Health. "Research Highlights: Helping Adolescents Resist Drugs." http://www.rand.org/pubs/ research_briefs?RB4518-1/index1.html

p. 102, par. 4, RAND Drug Policy Research Center. "News Release: Most Benefits From School-based Anti-Drug Efforts Come From Cuts in Tobacco and Alcohol Use, Not Street Drugs," http://www.rand.org

p. 103, par. 1, Brian Braiker, "Just Say Know—An Advocate of Drug Law Reform Says D.A.R.E. Is a 20-Year Old Failure," *Newsweek,* http://www.gangwar.com/items28.htm

p. 103, par. 3, Pierre Mezinski with Melissa Daly and Francoise Jaud, *Drugs Explained: The Real Deal on Alcohol, Pot, Ecstasy, and More,* p. 96.

p. 104, par. 3, University of Virginia, "21st Birthday Program Report for 2003–2004." http://www.virginia.edu/case/education/21st-birthday-card-report-2004.pdf

p. 104, par. 4, United States Department of Health and Human Services, Substance Abuse and Mental Health Services Administration (SAMHSA), "Binge Drinking in Adolescents and College Students," http://www.heath.org/govpubs/rpo995

p. 105, par. 3, Meredith Maran, *Dirty: A Search for Answers Inside America's Teenage Drug Epidemic,* p. 283.

p. 106, par. 3, Peter. D. Hart Research Associates, Inc. "Changing Public Attitudes toward the Criminal Justice System." http://www.soros.org/initiatives/justice/articles_publications/

p. 106, par. 5, Ibid.

121

FURTHER INFORMATION

Books

Beckman, Chris. *Clean: A New Generation in Recovery Speaks Out.* Center City, MN: Hazelden, 2005.

Esherick, Joan. *Dying for Acceptance: A Teen's Guide to Drug and Alcohol-Related Health Issues.* Philadelphia: Mason Crest Publishers, 2003.

Henderson, Harry. *Drug Abuse. Library in a Book.* New York: Facts on File, Inc., 2005.

Hyde, Margaret O., and John F. Setaro. *Drugs 101: An Overview for Teens.* Brookfield, CT: Twenty-First Century Press, 2003.

Maran, Meredith. *Dirty: A Search for Answers Inside America's Teenage Drug Epidemic.* New York: HarperCollins Publishers, 2003.

Mezinski, Pierre, with Melissa Daly and Francoise Jaud. *Drugs Explained: The Real Deal on Alcohol, Pot, Ecstasy, and More.* New York: Amulet Books, 2004.

Pinsky, Drew, with Todd Gold. *Cracked: Putting Broken Lives Together Again—A Doctor's Story.* New York: HarperCollins Publishers, 2003.

Organizations and Web Sites

Alanon/Alateen: Alanon helps families and friends recover from the effects of living with problem drinkers; Alateen is the recovery program for young people.

http://www.al-anon.alateen.org

Freevibe: a Web site for youth developed by the White House Office of National Drug Control Policy.

http://www.freevibe.com

Marijuana Anonymous Online: Internet resource for support, information, and recovery from marijuana addiction.

http://www.na-online.org

Monitoring the Future: an ongoing study of the behaviors, attitudes, and values of American young people; funded by the National Institute on Drug Abuse and conducted by the Institute for Social Research at the University of Michigan.

http://www.monitoringthefuture.org.

National Institute on Drug Abuse (NIDA) for Teens: Web site offering science-based information about how drugs affect the brain and body.

SMART Recovery: Self Management and Recovery Training, a four-step alternative to Alcoholics Anonymous and Narcotics Anonymous.

http://www.smartrecovery.org

BIBLIOGRAPHY

Adler, Jerry. "Toxic Strength." *Newsweek,* December 20, 2004, p. 44.

Aerosmith, with Stephen Davis. *Walk This Way: The Autobiography of Aerosmith.* New York: Avon Books, 1997.

American Civil Liberties Union. "ACLU Complaint in *SSDP v. Spellings,*" March 21, 2006. http://www.aclu.org/drugpolicy/gen/ (accessed June 27, 2006).

Beckman, Chris. *Clean: A New Generation in Recovery Speaks Out.* Center City, MN: Hazelden, 2005.

Boyum, David, and Mark A. R. Kleiman. "Breaking the Drug-Crime Link." *Public Interest,* Summer 2003.

Braiker, Brian. "Just Say Know—An Advocate of Drug Law Reform Says D.A.R.E. Is a 20-Year Old Failure." *Newsweek* Web Exclusive. http://www.gangwar.com/items28.htm (accessed July 19, 2006).

Carroll, Jamuna, ed. *Marijuana: Opposing Viewpoints.* Farmington Hills, MI: Greenhaven Press, 2005.

Carroll, Linda. "Marijuana's Effects: More Than Munchies." *New York Times,* January 29, 2002.

Chicago Sun-Times. "Study: Most Sexual Assaults Involve Drugs," May 11, 2006. http://www.suntimes.com (accessed May 15, 2000).

Childress, Sarah. "My Mother the Narc: Do Home Drug-Testing Kits Help or Hurt Teens?" *Newsweek,* April 10, 2006.

"Chocolate." http://www.chocolate.org (accessed June 13, 2006).

Collier, James. *Louis Armstrong: An American Genius.* New York: Oxford University Press, 1983.

"Crime as Business: The Career of Drug Dealer in a Brooklyn HousingProject."www.children/smartlibrary.org/NewInterface/segment/cfm?segment=1709 (accessed May 29, 2006).

DiConsiglio, John. "The High Road: Amanda Used to Smoke Marijuana and Then Drive a Car." *Scholastic Choices,* April–May 2006.

DiConsiglio, John. "Meth-Head Confession, *Scholastic Choices,* September, 2005.

Dodd, David. *Playing It Straight: Personal Conversations on Recovery, Transformation, and Success.* Deerfield Beach, FL: Health Communications, Inc., 1996.

Drugstory. "Muscle Madness: The Ugly Connection Between Body Image and Steroid Abuse." http://www.drugstory.org/feature/drugs_doping.asp

Fenway Community Health. "Personal Stories." http://www.fenwayhealth.org/site/PageServer?pagename=CM_ps_personalstories (accessed August 6, 2006).

Forte, Craig, LCSW. "A Harm Reduction Approach to Treating Problem Adolescent Alcohol Use." Clinical Social Work Society, http://www.clinicalsocialworksoety.org/documents/HarmReductionApproach.doc (accessed August 7, 2006).

Frontline, "Drug Wars," October 9–10, 2000. http://www.pbs.org/wgbh/pages/frontline/shows/drugs/buyers/socialhistory.html (accessed August 16, 2006).

Frontline, "Snitch," January 12, 1999. http://www.pbs.org/wgbh/pages/ frontline/shows/snitch/ (accessed July 2, 2006).

Gahlinger, Paul, *Illegal Drugs: A Complete Guide to Their History, Chemistry, Use, and Abuse.* New York: Plume, 2004.

Georgetown University Center for the Brain Basis of Cognition. "Spotlight on Dr. Nora Volkow." http://cbbc.georgetown.adu/on_campus_2004.html (accessed June 16, 2006).

Hansen, Nicole. "Real Drugs, False Friends," Partnership for a Drug-Free America. http://www.drugfree.org.Teen/teen_1.htm. (accessed Aug. 2, 2006).

Hart, Peter. D. Research Associates, Inc. "Changing Public Attitudes Toward the Criminal Justice System." Feb. 2002. http://www.soros.org/initiatives/justice/articles_publications/ (accessed July 12, 2006).

Henderson, Harry. *Drug Abuse.* Library in a Book. New York: Facts on File, Inc., 2005.

Hyde, Margaret O., and John F. Setaro. *Drugs 101: An Overview for Teens.* Brookfield, CT: Twenty-First Century Press, 2003.

Kaiser, Jocelyn. "New Head of Drug Institute is Wired for Action." *Science,* July 4, 2003.

Kiedis, Anthony. *Scar Tissue.* New York: Hyperion, 2004.

Light, Alan. "Out of Their Tree: Red Hot Chili Peppers," *Spin,* May 2006.

MacMillan, Leigh. "Imaging Reveals Secrets of Addiction: Brain Awareness Keynote Lecture," *The Reporter,* Vanderbilt Medical Center, March 21, 2003. http://www.mc.vanderbilt.edu/reporter/index.html

Maran, Meredith. *Dirty: A Search for Answers Inside America's Teenage Drug Epidemic.* New York: HarperCollins, 2003.

Marijuana Anonymous. www.marijuanaanonymous.org/Pages/teens. html (accessed May 30, 2006).

Markert, John. "Sing a Song of Drug Use-Abuse: Four Decades of Drug Lyrics in Popular Music—From the Sixties through the Nineties." *Sociological Inquiry,* Spring 2001.

Marlatt, G. Alan. "Harm Reduction Works." *Alcohol Problems and Solutions.* http://www2.Potsdam.edu/hansondj/YouthIssues/index.html (accessed August 5, 2006).

Mezinski, Pierre, with Melissa Daly and Francoise Jaud. *Drugs Explained: The Real Deal on Alcohol, Pot, Ecstasy, and More.* New York: Amulet Books, 2004.

Narconon Southern California. "Drug Rehab a Tough Lesson." January 27, 2005. http://www.addictionca.com/newsleft.htm?aid=422 (accessed August 1, 2006).

National Campaign to Prevent Teen Pregnancy. "Sex and Drugs." January 2003. http://www.teenpregnancy.org/resources/reading/fact_sheets/drugsondcp.asp (accessed June 7, 2006).

National Center on Addiction and Substance Abuse (CASA) at Columbia University. "National Survey of American Attitudes on Substance Abuse X: Teens and Parents." August 2005. http://www.casacolumbia.org (accessed May 30, 2006).

——. "New Study in Archives of Pediatrics and Adolescent Medicine and CASA Report Reveal: Underage Drinkers, Alcoholics, and Alcohol Abusers Consume Between 37.5 and 48.8 Percent of Alcohol Sold." http://www.casacolumbia.org/absolutenm/templates/PressReleases.aspx?articleide=437&zoneid=56b (accessed August 15, 2006).

——. *Women Under the Influence.* Baltimore, MD: Johns Hopkins University Press, 2006.

National Institute on Drug Abuse. "The Brain & Addiction." http://teens.drugabuse.gov/facts/facts_brain2.asp (accessed June 4, 2006).

Nestler, Eric J., and Robert C. Malenka. "The Addicted Brain." *Scientific American,* March 2004.

Northwestern University. "Measuring Brain Activity in People Eating Chocolate Offers New Clues About How the Body Becomes Addicted," http://www.nwu.edu. (accessed June 13, 2006). Also: http://www.chocolate.org/choclove/index.html. [This site has the Northwestern report.]

O'Bryan, Nicole, as told to Cecilia Goodnow. "I was addicted to crystal meth." *CosmoGIRL!,* May 2004.

Office of Juvenile Justice and Delinquency Prevention. "Substance Abuse: The Nation's Number One Health Problem." OJJDP Fact Sheet, May 2001 (accessed June 7, 2006).

Office of National Drug Control Police. "Girls and Drugs," Feb. 9, 2006 http://www.mediacampaign.org/newsroom/press06/020906.html

——"Substance in Popular Movies and Music." http://www.mediacampaign.org/ publications/movies/movie_partII.html (accessed May 25, 2006).

——."Substance Use in Popular Prime-Time Television." http://www.mediacampaign.org/publications/primetime/television_summa ry.html. (accessed May 25, 2006).

——."Teens, Drugs, and Driving: Steer Clear of Pot." http://www.mediacampaign.org/steerclear/factsheet.html (accessed July 4, 2006).

Parents. The Anti-Drug. "My Big Brother Is a Meth Addict," posted by Tina on October 17, 2005. http://www.theantidrug.com/community/ktopics.asp?topic=3 (accessed May 30, 2006).

Partnership for a Drug-Free America. "Agony from Ecstasy." http://www.drugfree.org/Teen/teen2.html (accessed May 30, 2006).

Partnership for a Drug-Free America. "I Could Never Get High Enough." http://www.drugfree.org/General/Stories/display story.aspx?id (accessed May 16, 2006).

Partnership for a Drug free America. "My 17th Birthday." http://www.drugfree.org/Portal/Stories/My_17th_Birthday_ (accessed May 30, 2006).

Penny, Denise. "Cuckoo for Cocoa?" *New York* magazine, November 1, 2004. http://newyorkmetro.com/nymetro/ urban/ strategist/everything/chocolate/10188/(accessed June 13, 2006).

Phillips, Lauren. "Fewer Drugs on Television—Media Contains More Drug References." January 19, 2000. http://www.stanford daily.com/article/2000/1/19/fewer/DrugsOnTelevisionMedia ContainsMoreDrugReferences (accessed August 17, 2006).

Psychology Today. "Inside the Addict's Brain." http://www. psychologytoday.com/articles/pto-19940901-000022.html (accessed July 16, 2006).

RAND Corporation. "Treatment: Effective (But Unpopular) Weapon Against Drugs." Spring 1995. http://www.rand.org/publications/randreview/issues/RRR.spring95.crime/treatment.html (accessed July 16, 2006).

RAND Drug Policy Research Center. "Assessing U.S. Drug Problems and Policy," 2005. http://www.rand.org (accessed July 12, 2006).

——."News Release: Most Benefits From School-based Anti-Drug Efforts Come From Cuts in Tobacco and Alcohol Use, Not Street Drugs," December 11, 2002. http://www.rand.org (accessed July 19, 2006).

RAND Health. "Research Highlights: Helping Adolescents Resist Drugs." http://www.rand.org/pubs/research_briefs?RB45181/index1.html (accessed July 19, 2006).

Roleff, Tamara L., ed. *Drug Abuse: Opposing Viewpoints.* Farmington Hills, MI: Greenhaven Press, 2005.

Rutledge, Raquel. "Drug Wars Being Fought at Home: Parents Test their Teens More Often." *Milwaukee Journal Sentinel*, March 6, 2006. http://www.jsonline.com (accessed June 9, 2006).

Shapiro, Harry. *Waiting for the Man: The Story of Drugs and Popular Music.* London: Helter Skelter Publishing, 1999.

SMART Recovery. http://www.smartrecovery.org. (accessed July 19, 2006).

Smith, Larry. "10 Questions About Pot," *Teen People,* April 1, 2003.

Sterling, Eric E., and Julie Stewart. "Undo the Legacy of Len Bias's Death." *Washington Post,* June 24, 2006.

Syndistar Inc. Educational Publishers. "The Refusal Challenge." http://www.intheknowzone.com/whattosay/testresults.asp (accessed May 31, 2006).

Szalavitz, Maia. "The Trouble with Tough Love." *Washington Post,* January 29, 2006. http://www.slate.com/id/2076329 (accessed July 22, 2006).

——"Trick or Treatment: Teen Drug Programs Turn Curious Teens Into Crackheads." *Slate,* January 3, 2003.

Taber, Andrew. "Roid Rage." *Salon,* November 18, 1999. http://www.salon.com/health/feature/199/11/18/steroids/index.html (accessed May 23, 2006).

Travis, Alan, and Sally James Gregory. "How Rock 'n' Roll Fell Out of Love with Drugs." *The Guardian,* October 27, 2003. http://arts.guardian.co.uk/news/ story/0,11711,1071720,00.html (accessed April 12, 2006).

United States Bureau of Justice Statistics. http://www.ojp.usdoj.gov/bjs/dcf/du.htm

United States Department of Health and Human Services, Substance Abuse and Mental Health Services Administration (SAMHSA). "Binge Drinking in Adolescents and College Students." http://www,heath.org/govpubs/rpo995 (accessed August 15, 2006).

United States Department of Justice, Office of Justice Programs. *Drug Courts: The Second Decade,* June 2006. http://www.ojp.usddoj.gov/nij (accessed July 3, 2006).

University of Michigan Institute for Social Research. "Monitoring the Future: National Results on Adolescent Drug Use." Overview of Key Findings, 2005.

University of Virginia. "21st Birthday Card Project Report for 2003-2004." http://www.virginia.edu/case/education/21st-birthday-card-report-2004.pdf (accessed August 15, 2006).

Von Zielbauer, Paul. "Court Treatment System Is Found to Help Drug Offenders Stay Clean." *The New York Times,* November 9, 2003. http://www.nytimes.com (accessed July 5, 2006).

White House Office of National Drug Control Policy. "Drug Courts." http://www.whitehousedrugpolicy/gov/enforce/drugcourt.html (accessed July 3, 2006).

——."The Economic Costs of Drug Abuse in the United States, 1992–2002. Executive Summary." http://www.whitehousedrugpolicy.gov/publications/index.html (accessed July 8, 2006).

Wolf, Elaine. "Everyday Hassles: Barriers to Recovery in Drug Court." *Journal of Drug Issues*, Winter 2001. http://www.find articles.com (accessed July 3, 2006).

Zoler, Mitchel L. "History Flags Teen Drug Abuse Better Than a Drug Test," *Family Practice News,* March 1, 2001.

INDEX

Page numbers in **boldface** are illustrations, tables, and charts.

ABOUT THE AUTHOR

Joan Axelrod-Contrada is the author of several books for middle school and high school students. She has written about a variety of topics, including women leaders, the Lizzie Borden trail, colonial America, and freedom of speech on the Internet. She is currently at work on a new book for Marshall Cavendish Benchmark about the landmark case of *Plessy* v. *Ferguson* ("separate but equal"). She and her husband, Fred, a newspaper reporter, are the parents of two teenage children, Amanda and Rio.